To

and adviser and

Thank you!

Laleh

UNDER
THE VEIL

ISLAM'S SHROUDED SECRET

UNDER THE VEIL

ISLAM'S SHROUDED SECRET

BY LALEH AZHADI

Edited & Designed by Sarah I. ClarkNova

Cover Photo: (http://www.dhushara.com/book/sakina/fatwah/purdah.htm)

Printed in the United States of America

First Printing: May 2010

ISBN--978-0-557-45164-7

TABLE OF CONTENTS

ACKNOWLEDGEMENT

I would like to express my deepest gratitude to my daughter, who saw me through this book by providing not only her moral support, but also her knowledge in editing, proofreading, design, and publishing. She has also been invaluable for bouncing off ideas and offering her comments and experiences.

I would like to thank my friends for their moral support and to-the-point feedback and suggestions. They have continued to remind me of the necessity of viewing Hijab as a time critical subject.

Above all, I want to thank my husband, who supported and encouraged me to complete this book, as well as his many trips to the library to pick up documents for my research.

INTRODUCTION

"The hottest place in Hell is reserved for those

who remain neutral in times of moral crisis."

Dante Alighieri

We are now in the Twenty-First century, thousands of moons away from Mohammad's vision of the Archangel Gabriel proclaiming him to be the Messenger of *Allah*. It was 610 A.D. when Gabriel appeared to him in a cave and murmured the words of the Koran. He called his religion Islam. One of the meanings of this word is 'peace,' but it would seem that there has been anything but peace since Islam's emergence, particularly for Muslim women.

My purpose in writing this book is to examine some of Islam's laws, cultures, and practices, both written and unwritten, largely relating to women. Fourteen hundred years have passed since Islam's inception and my key question remains – have the lives of millions of Islamic women improved? This book examines the daily existence of young girls and women who have no choice but to live by antiquated religious, cultural, and tribal practices – and conversely, an examination of modern Muslim women who do have a choice.

Growing up in the Islamic culture of Iran meant living with restrictions and somewhat unbreakable rules. I was blessed with an investigative mind and was raised in a competitive family environment without Hijab, the Islamic head cover for women.

I do have my share of complaints about my upbringing, mainly that I did not have the freedom to do things by myself or choose my friends and social settings – but years later, after leaving Iran, I realized how fortunate I was with the few freedoms I had.

The 1979 Iranian Islamic Revolution, which took away most of women's freedoms, along with their ability to make decisions for themselves or their children, opened my eyes and adjusted my way of thinking. For the first time, I was able to describe my male family members as progressive in comparison to millions of other Muslim men who create constant anguish for the women in their families.

The notion of living as a second-class citizen may be hard to grasp and is certainly a foreign concept for most of us in the

Western world, but imagine the worst situation at the peak of African slavery in the United States and then extend the duration to thousands of years – centuries of hopelessness and stagnation. Generations of women in Islamic societies have quietly suffered and survived in these conditions.

Muslim women's suffering is certainly a dark stain on the history of humanity. Their right to free speech and freedom of movement is a just cause but without a single champion. Faceless victims have no voice and are brutalized daily.

Few outside the Muslim world would disagree that grave injustices are being committed towards women, however, the silence and inaction that most of us are guilty of speaks volumes about our lack of understanding of the crimes, or inability or unwillingness to affect the positive changes needed to end Islam's heinous practices. This cause, like other just causes throughout the history of humanity, requires the collective effort of all races, genders, and lifestyles to unite, assess the problem, and seek short and long-term solutions. We must free battered women from the hands of bullies and tyrants by giving women a future appropriate for today's life-style and worthy of the meaning of the word 'civilization.'

The Pre-Islamic Republican Revolution

Although most are aware of the enforced rule of Hijab[1] after Iran's 1979 Islamic Revolution, many people do not know about the strange twist of history that happened a few generations before. During the Pahlavi Dynasty (1925 – 1979)[2], Reza Shah Pahlavi, who ruled until 1941, took drastic measures against Islamic fundamentalism and actually banned women from wearing Hijab in public. He created an extensive system of secular primary and secondary schools and, in 1935, established the country's first European-style university in Tehran. Reza shah also expanded the roads including the completion of the railroad, and established state-owned factories to produce goods such as textiles, matches, canned goods, sugar, and cigarettes. His actions were designed to break then, current religious autonomy including breaking the religious sect's monopoly on education. By creating a body of secular law and judiciary system, he further limited power of the clerics. He created secular court systems outside of clerics' judgeships.

---

[1] Hijab – The general term for the Islamic head covering.

[2] The Pahlavi Dynasty ruled Iran from the crowning of Reza Shah Pahlavi in 1925 to the overthrow of his son Mohammad Reza Pahlavi in the Iranian Revolution of 1979.

I can only imagine the hard feelings that developed among the *mullahs* (Islamic clergy) as a result of Reza Shah's actions.

As a young radical Shiite clergyman living in religious city of Qum, Ayatollah Khomeini turned into one of the most active oppositionists against the Shah. Khomeini's crusade against the Pahlavi Dynasty went on for decades, which eventually led to the overthrow of the Pahlavi heir Mohammed Reza Shah, widely known as the Shah of Iran.

During Pahlavi rule, women benefited from relative freedom and advanced in several socioeconomic areas such as politics, finance, education, and medicine. Women attended universities, entered into public life and, for the first time in centuries, were able to travel abroad without asking for permission from their husbands.

Conversely, I remember the stories that my maternal grandmother shared about those days, which she referred to as the 'Dark Time.' A young woman during Reza Shah's reign, my grandmother had been brought up to wear Hijab and believed it was the only appropriate way a woman of her family status should appear in public. Reza Shah's law, which forbade women from appearing in public wearing a *chador* (the long, black veil favored as Hijab in Iran) or headscarf, was a drastic swing from the status quo of the time, ultimately causing disgrace to millions of women like my grandmother. Refusal to obey the Shah's law could have severe consequences, including confrontation with the local police or jail time.

My grandmother and other women in her family stayed home for months at a time and did not risk going out in public. In her view, she would have shamed her family by going out in attire in which men could see her hair and the shape of her body.

Eventually, the ban was lifted and women like my grandmother were again able to appear in public wearing a scarf and modest clothing, thus enabling them to rejoin society in a way they considered appropriate and safe.

Iranian newspaper clip from 1968 reading: "A quarter of Iran's Nuclear Energy scientists are women." (En.wikipedia.org)

Years later, during my own childhood, my mother and I would see a mixed bag of appearances on Iranian streets, from the *chador* to scarves or bare heads. Of course, certain places, such as religious gatherings and mosques, required women to enter with proper Hijab.

It seems ridiculous that so much controversy would be generated over a piece of cloth covering a woman's head. Logic dictates that women themselves should decide their own mode of dress in a way that is appropriate to their environment and cultural setting. Traditional women generally wear some form of Hijab as a cultural custom rather than as a forced religious ruling.

Although Hijab refers to a certain mode of dress, that definition only scratches the surface. Right alongside the rules of Hijab are many other unjust rules imposed upon Muslim women.

I asked my daughter, a college-educated woman born and raised in the United States, to describe her childhood memory of Hijab:

I flashed back to the Mosque and Islamic School classes with dad. What I remember most clearly was the different namaz *[prayer] rooms for men and women. The men had a spacious, high-ceilinged hall with beautiful light green carpet, an attractive altar in the middle where the Imam would sit, and plenty of copies of the Koran placed on ornate, carved wooden book holders. There were silk flowers, framed images of Islamic art and other such decorations. The room always seemed cool, with fresh air, and it was a fairly attractive place to be. Unlike most girls, I had some limited access to the men's hall. Because I was still a young girl of nine or ten, with no female relative or guardian at the Mosque, I was permitted to go in there if I needed to speak with my dad.*

In contrast, the women's namaz *room was cramped and overly warm, an upstairs loft overlooking the men's hall through minaret-shaped cutouts in the wall. Although I was a child and my spatial sense was surely exaggerated, I remember the women's room as being about 1/10 of the size of the hall occupied by the men. All the women and children sat with their prayer mats literally touching each other, sweaty in the stuffy air.*

Just getting up to that room was a dreaded trek: up a few flights of stairs in a dark, stuffy stairwell, through a brown-carpeted foyer and then into the crowded room itself. I always dreaded namaz.

Even as a child I wondered why they couldn't simply draw a curtain down the middle of the men's hall and put women on one side and men on the other. My dad explained to me that women must always stand behind men. This, I thought, was ridiculous.

School girls during the Pahlavi Dynasty in Iran. (Irandokht.com)

MY QUEST AND OBLIGATION

Perhaps not unlike many of you, I am a lifelong learner. My quest for knowledge is not confined to life's mundane issues such as our national economy, healthcare reform, or the price of gasoline. Rather, I discovered a deep and abiding interest – nay, obsession – with the Islamic practice of Hijab: the practice of female concealment from men.

Along the way, I began to form many questions that I strove to address about this religion and the practice of Hijab:

1) Who decided that the same little boy hiding under his mother's skirt would act as an Islamic fashion authority by designing women's wardrobes when he became a man?

2) Why is it women's clothing that defines a society's level of modesty and integrity? And is this really the only motivation behind the enforcement of Hijab by Muslim men? Are billions of non-Hijab wearing women living in societies without modesty and integrity?

3) Are modern Hijab-wearing women and their advocates conscious of the millions of oppressed Muslim women around the globe? Can these modern women see a connection between their chosen act of promoting Hijab and the inability of millions of Muslim women to speak out for themselves and their preferences?

4) If wearing Hijab is a direct instruction from the Koran, and since there is only one Koran and one set of rules for core practices, why does the appearance of Hijab differ from culture to culture?

5) How many centuries does it take for an idea or ideology to fail its people before it is declared obsolete?

6) As is referenced in the Koran and The Prophet's *Hadiths*, where do we find the verses speaking of peace and harmony among people of all nations?

7) Realistically speaking, are not peace-loving Muslims chasing a chimera as long as Islam predominately speaks of destroying the infidels and promoting *jihad?*

In my journey to a deeper understanding of the practices, differences and basis of Hijab, I discovered a wealth of pedagogy, demagoguery, misinformation, righteous religious indignation, and downright falsehoods, all of which I have had difficulty comprehending. Further, I have discovered my own passion for the cause of the millions of women who constantly strain under the yolk of male oppression in the Islamic world. I have become aware of my obligation to this community of women, realizing that it is up to the able women in the world to help uplift those who are not so able.

There are many peace-loving people who believe that everyone can make their own choice to live a happy life, but I believe wholeheartedly that despite a deep desire to live in peace and harmony, the oppressed women in the Islamic nations have been deprived of their fundamental human rights, thus making it impossible to simply choose a life of peace. It is up to the rest of us to unveil the truth and expose the ongoing injustices and crimes done to them. I consider it my duty as a woman and a citizen of this world to help my underprivileged and tyrannized sisters across the globe.

A New Generation of Muslim Women

I would like to clarify that in this book I am not directing my words to the grandmothers and elders of conservative Islamic societies, but to the young women growing up therein. I also speak to women living in Western societies who have made a conscious decision not only to wear Hijab but also to endorse it as a tool to guide women to a so-called state of liberation and independence. And finally, I am speaking to men of all ages, living in Islamic and non-Islamic societies, who have an opinion on the subjugation of women, yet hesitate to express their dismay and continue to keep their silence.

Over the years, I have engaged in numerous conversations with progressive, conscientious men of all ages and lifestyles who express their frustration and anger towards the restrictions imposed on women by Islamic fundamentalism. Hijab is the beginning of a long series of restrictions with direct and indirect impact on women's daily lives and in order to arrive at solutions, I encourage diligent men to speak up and carry on with continuous dialogue about this subject.

I am also curious about the rationale in a young woman's mind that leads to using Hijab as a tool for liberation rather than as a hindrance to her mobility and physique. Is this a form of rebellion against the male dominance in her life or is it a calculated, in-depth decision? I am genuinely interested in knowing if these modern Islamic women, full of ideas and convictions, have dug deeply enough to realize the daily consequences of their actions against the miserable lives of the millions of women who are forced to live with Hijab.

Growing up in Iran, I often witnessed situations in which women were treated as compliant sex objects. Women were victims of pinching and fondling on the streets, or simply disrespected by the men in their families. They were portrayed as hysterical, brainless characters in local movies and theatre shows.

I did not comprehend the reasoning behind the constant belittling of women through verbal abuse, rules, hitting, and shouting. They were mistreated as mindless and soulless objects, like old rags, which could be thrown away at the owners' will.

Throughout my life, I mostly heard from men and *mullahs* (Islamic clergy) that Paradise belongs to faithful women and obedient mothers and wives. Is it not rational to conclude that if obedient women go to Paradise, the tyrants and oppressors of women must go to a fiery hell?

In some countries, it is customary for women in the family to cook and serve men of the family first, and only eat the leftovers after the men have finished and left the room.

It is also still customary for Muslim men to call upon their wives using the name of her firstborn son. I remember my maternal grandfather, a man of Islam, calling my grandmother by her first son's name, 'Ali'. Unfortunately, it is too late to confront or educate my grandfather on his injustice and ask my grandmother how she felt about this. They both passed away long before I became conscious that there was any injustice at all. I can only hope that they have both gone to a place with fewer classifications and restrictions.

Calling a woman by her first son's name is not a religious practice, but is customary in the same cultures that foster Islam. Although it may be pleasing and even romantic at first, losing one's identity and self-value, may take its toll and over time destroy a woman's spirit. It is beyond my comprehension how a so-called liberated, modern Islamic woman can rationalize the concept of her mother, sister or grandmother losing her identity to a first-born son.

In Islamic societies, everything begins and ends with male honor. Once I began to analyze and peel away the layers, honor was the common denominator surfacing time and time again and it was always related to some form of sexuality, whether a woman's body or a man's appetite for physical pleasure. Centuries old teachings have persuaded women to fear the consequences if they rebel against their traditional and religious status quo. There is a deep-rooted evil genius in this behavior, which isolates half the population from wanting to seek pleasure for fear of reprimand, with the other half seizing whatever they want at anytime they please, and having the force of law to back them up.

I have a deep sense of resentment toward those who would hinder the development of women, and in particular those who would prevent the growth of Muslim women's sense of self and self-esteem by promoting a system of oppression, torture, desperation, and hopelessness among the millions of Muslim women around the world.

CHAPTER I

HIJAB

"How could anyone defend [the veil] as preserving anything but the low regard and true unimportance of women... [a veiled] woman is a walking billboard that proclaims public space is reserved for men [and that]a woman's place is indoors."

Jennifer Hurley (Islam – Opposing Viewpoints)

THE MEANING OF HIJAB

According to the Merriam Webster Dictionary, the Arabic word Hijab is defined as: *"the traditional covering for the hair and neck that is worn by Muslim women."* The word is also used to refer to the modest, body-covering dresses or jackets worn by Muslim women when outside their homes and at any time when they are in the presence of men not closely related to them.

Hijab comes in many different forms, but always covers the woman's head. The customary form in Iran is a cloak-like piece of black cloth called a *chador*. In Arab countries, Hijab consists of the *chador* with the addition of a face covering called *niqab,* through which only the eyes can be seen. The *burqa* is the garment in Afghanistan, covering the entire body from head to toe with only a small rectangular net allowing limited vision.

An example of *niqab.* (Themuslimwoman.org)

In the book, *Islam – Opposing Viewpoints,* Canadian writer Michelle Lemon indicates that, whether or not Islam has granted equal rights to women, local clergy and *mullahs* have imposed their own interpretation of Hijab, which is anchored in their personal understandings of the Koran in conjunction with regional customs and values.

The key question is whether Hijab is meant to protect women's chastity or to control their movements and separate them from the free world. Are all Islamic men, including the Prophet himself, so possessed by an uncontrollable urge to satisfy their lust that they need women to be covered? The abundance of laws governing Hijab has obviously not contributed to the further development of the Islamic nations. Many people are still distressed, confused, and hungry for sex and sexuality.

Hijab creates anonymity among women: they become faceless and nameless, property of fathers and husbands. Women in Hijab are not permitted to raise their voices or laugh in public. Islamic men claim that women's hair is a kind of magical stimulant arousing men's sexual appetites. My question is a simple one: where is the scientific research differentiating the DNA of male and female hair, isolating a chemical compound correlating to men's sexual organs? This idea is clearly absurd. The entire tradition of Hijab has been created around men's pleasure and control – or lack thereof.

Islam has expressed its low opinion of women in the Koran, the *Hadiths* (the sayings of the Prophet as told by his disciples), and the teachings of the clergy. It considers women to be inferior to men anatomically, academically, emotionally, and ethically. Therefore, more progressive societies must consider Islam as deeply anti-woman. Do not be surprised to find misogynistic sayings, such as: *"If anything presages a bad omen it is: a house, a woman, a horse."* Or, *"Never will a people know success if they confide their affairs to a woman."*

Iranian women wearing the traditional *chador*.

"Hejaab" by Please! Don't Smile.

(Distributed through the Creative Commons 3.0 License)

In *Women in Islam*, the author refers to the Koranic emphasis on women's natural inferiority, claiming that women are physically and intellectually weaker than men are, and that women are impure and less devoted because they cannot carry out their religious duties while menstruating. Because of this, women are considered incapable of leadership.

Conscientious people must argue against Islam's granting the rights of decision-making and guardianship to men. *"Men are in charge of women, because Allah hath made the one of them to excel the other."* (Koran, 4:34) It may be stated in the Koran, but it makes no sense in our modern times.

Men's Reactions to Hijab

"The only thing necessary for the triumph [of evil]

is for good men to do nothing."

Edmund Burke

Without a doubt, there are millions of Islamic men silently laughing at the Koran and *Hadiths*, which place women's fate in the hands of men. From chastity to finance, from fashion to life and death, without a doubt, it is men who make the decisions. Koranic laws and *Hadiths* state that a woman's legal testimony is only worth half that of a man's and that woman inherit only half of a man's share of wealth.

While Islam holds no one responsible for someone else's wrongdoing, fundamentalists hold women accountable for the potential misdeeds of men and require them to veil themselves in order to prevent the encouragement of vulgar thoughts. Consequently, women are destined to stay inside their homes, raise their children, and obey their husbands. The Prophet only grants women freedom from wearing Hijab while they are in the company of their husbands, fathers, sons or husband's sons, brothers, nephews, other women, slaves (including male servants who have been castrated), and finally small children who have no sense of sexual embarrassment.

This uncontrollable male obsession with female sexuality is shameful and degrading, not only for women but also for the men themselves. I am mystified and puzzled by the absence of reaction from men who have not lost their sanity to this mockery masterminded by the Prophet and the Islamic clergy.

Now, more than any other time in the history, it is the duty of conscientious men to speak up against these cruel rulings and demeaning laws forced on women in the name of Islam. Men and women must unite to confront the Islamic fanatics and clergy who echo the antiquated rulings of the Koran, *Hadiths*, and other Islamic laws limiting women's travel, autonomy, literacy, financial and family decisions and place of residence without needing permission from men in the family; fathers, brothers, husbands and sons.

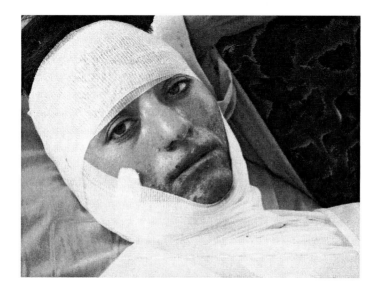

Domestic violence forces some Afghan women into "self-immolations, suicide, escape from home, forced prostitution, and addiction to narcotics." (Photo: Khaled Nahiz/IRIN, February 11, 2010 – Irinnews.org)

Women's Reactions to Hijab

The people most affected by Hijab are also the ones who are not allowed to speak out against it. Although Hijab refers to a head covering, there is much suffering hidden beneath. Muslim women in support of Hijab need to confront this subject with sincerity. They must step outside of their environment and step into the world of millions of women whose fate has been chosen for them. There are women right now committing the most brutal form of suicide by setting themselves on fire in a desperate attempt to free themselves from their daily despair. These are hopeless, faceless, and nameless women and girls held in a sort of slavery by the men in their family in the name of Islam and *Allah,* "the benevolent."

Is Hijab a Local Custom? The *Burqa*

Former King of Afghanistan, Amanullah Khan[1], led his country to independence from the United Kingdom and attempted to liberate Afghani women from wearing the *burqa*. He asked the clergy to find instructions in the Koran referring to the *burqa* and they were

---

[1] King *Amanullah Khan (1919-1929)* Born. June 1, 1892 – died April 25, 1960.

apparently unable to find such passages. Only three sections in the Koran reference clothing:[1] 1) asking for men and women to dress appropriately, 2) advising the Prophet to direct female believers to cover their lower neck and cleavage, and 3) asking Mohammad's wives to lower their voices, dress properly, stay home, and avoid showing off their beauty in public.

The Afghani style *burqa* is a circular shaped textile, which covers a woman's body from head to toe and has an embroidered opening in front of the face, allowing limited vision and imparting a ghostly impression. The author of *Women and the Koran* writes:

…the effect of all these garments is the same, though; for the woman is rendered anonymous, a non-person, unapproachable, just a silent being skulking along, looking neither to the right or left. To those who do not know her personally, she is nameless and faceless. She is also marked as a taboo that no one dares to approach her or talk to her. (Hekmat, 1997)

---

[1] Koran: 7:26; An-Nur 24:31; Al-Ahzab 33:59.

A woman holds her child under her *burqa*. Her daughter, with a simple headscarf, is not yet of the required age to wear the *burqa*.

("Women Going to the Vegetable Market" by N_Creatures /

Distributed under the Creative Commons 2.5 License)

Physicians for Human Rights have reported that as a result of wearing *burqa*, women were endangering their eyesight and hearing and have had a higher incidence of skin rashes, breathing problems, headaches, hair loss, depression, and heart problems. In addition, lack of exposure to sunshine denies women the proper amount of vitamin D, contributing to bone loss.

Hijab and Special Religious Patrols

After *Mullah* Mohammed Omar[1] took over Kabul, Afghanistan in 1996, he ordered all women to cease their outside jobs and stay inside their houses. Women had to have a pressing need to leave their homes and, even then, they had to be bundled up in *burqa* and accompanied by a man: husband, father, son, or brother. As *Mullah* Omar said, *"A woman's face corrupts men"*.

In Islamic countries around the globe, women face outright brutality at the hands of ruling men, all in the name of Hijab. Every day, thousands of women are assaulted, maimed, or killed for their refusal to abide by such pretenses. In Saudi Arabia, special religious patrols beat and abuse women for not wearing proper Hijab in public. In post-Taliban Afghanistan, women have been raped for daring to think they could now go without the *burqa*.

In *Veiled Threat*, Sally Armstrong describes a situation occurring on the streets of Kabul not too long ago, in which a woman who was being beaten by Taliban "watchdogs" for wearing nail polish,

---

[1] Mohammed Omar. Born c. 1959, Nodeh, near Kandahar. He was launched into the spotlight after the terror created in Sept, 11, 2001.

observed another woman's polished fingers being cut off by a group of Taliban men.

The Taliban enforced hundreds of rules, most of them written against women in order to keep them inside their houses and restrict their comings and goings, even forbidding women from going to parties, hotels, and restaurants. They carried out threats of punishment on anyone, such as shopkeepers or taxi drivers, who directly spoke and conducted business with women who were without the proper Hijab, the *burqa*.

Women in Afghanistan have been forgotten, feeling like the living dead and wondering about their shady and uncertain future.

My Mother's Experience

In Tehran, Iran in the early 1990s, the special religious patrols abducted my mother during her daily shopping. Without explanation, two women in *chador* (the Iranian Hijab) approached my mother and forced her into a mini bus parked on the intersection's corner. As she was pushed into the bus, she protested and asked the reason. Their answer was shocking: that she was wearing too much makeup. Angrily, she ran her fingers across her rose-colored face and held them up in front of the women, asking if they could find any trace of makeup on her fingers. She hurriedly explained to them that with her blue eyes and fair skin she could easily blush and look as if she had been made up.

Ignoring her, they left her in the bus and went back to the busy street to hunt down more victims. My mother situated herself in one of the seats and observed the other women snatched earlier by the patrols. Several hours later, many angry and frustrated women, including some young high school students, occupied the bus. The patrols did not respond to their pleas to allow a phone call to their parents or husbands to let them know of their whereabouts.

A long time passed before the bus started driving to an unknown destination. After more than half an hour of driving, they arrived at a deserted mansion on the outskirts of Tehran. The house had been occupied by the Iranian Revolutionary Guard, who had freely commandeered private property during the Islamic Revolution. Ushered inside the building, the women were made to sit on benches outside a large room that had been converted into a courtroom and was guarded by male and female patrols.

My mother and the other women were thirsty, hungry, and worried sick about their fate. No one answered their questions or offered them a phone call to their loved ones. After many hours passed, my mother was called into the courtroom where there was one *mullah* sitting behind the desk and a few others around him. The *mullah* looked my mother over, who had her hair covered with a large scarf and was wearing the proper clothing dictated by the Islamic Republic Government. He asked the patrolwomen for the reason behind my mother's abduction and after their explanation was heard, he quickly dismissed the case, as my mother was clearly wearing no makeup.

Without further delay or explanation, my mother was quickly ushered outside onto the adjacent street. She had no idea where she was or how to get home. The street was empty except for the patrol buses and the Revolutionary Guards' jeeps. No one offered her ride to the next busy intersection to catch a bus or taxi.

Meanwhile, my father was beside himself when he realized that my mother's shopping had taken several hours more than usual. He walked around the neighborhood, called friends and relatives, and shortly had several people driving around and calling hospitals looking for her as well.

By the time my mother walked to the busy main road and found public transportation to take her home, it was already night. Walking in, she discovered my father looking powerless and devastated, waiting for her arrival and praying for her safety.

Why is Hijab Not Standardized?

What is the Suffering as Result of Hijab?

Some so-called progressive Islamic women accuse the Western media of being obsessed with the dress code of Hijab. Pro-Hijab women maintain that they are not surrendering to male domination but that a woman's merit is more important than her clothing; we should pay more attention to her achievements than her Hijab. These modern Islamic women also criticize the media for focusing on the Afghani *burqa*, for example, rather than the need to educate Afghani women or help them feed their children.

Regrettably, the reality for millions of women living in Muslim countries is very different from the realities of those women who have the freedom to choose. The difference lies between choosing Hijab of their own free will or having it forced upon them. Educated Muslim women should understand that male-enforced Hijab is an act of domination over women's lives, bodies, and souls. The *burqa* and other forms of veiling are not the core issue if the choice to wear them is made entirely by the women themselves.

For centuries, however, it has been the men making these decisions. In this way, they signal society to treat women like children, minors, and mentally challenged individuals, by telling them what to do, how to behave, what to wear, and how to run their lives. Hijab establishes certain mannerisms, which have been designed, formulated, and dictated by men.

One can say that a religion forcing a dress code upon women is not democratic, and every aspect of a woman's freedom is stripped from her. In a democratic society, men and women possess certain freedoms, including the freedom to choose their wardrobe.

In societies where certain rules apply only to women, the enforcers hold entitlement and ownership over those women, and they don't stop only with clothing. They go on controlling other facets of women's lives, thereby encouraging illiteracy, honor killing, restricted traveling, and preventing women from making decisions for their children and themselves. Whether the blame resides with Islam or other factors, the outcome is the same. Men are abusing Islamic rules in general and Hijab in particular, to force their hegemony on women.

Women must question the reason behind Hijab. Women don't cover themselves in the company of their children or other women; Hijab is worn only around men. Why do women feel inadequate and exposed while they are in the presence of men? Is it because women are not able to control their behavior and modesty around men or do they cover themselves to protect men from potential misbehavior and wrongful thoughts? If women wear Hijab because, as the Koran says, *"men become aroused by looking at women's hair and body,"* aren't women deceiving themselves if they think that they have arrived at the decision to wear Hijab all on their own? The act alone demonstrates the wrongful influence and domination of men over women's decisions. If women have to stop and think how to dress, and dress in a certain manner dictated by men, then the action itself points to limitations imposed on women.

In a reasonable democratic or socialist society, men and women compromise and make sacrifices for each other to ensure their needs and desires are met. What is absent in Islamic societies is sensitivity to women's needs. We don't see men dressing a certain way for women or even bothering to discover what interests and stimulates them. As long as mutual collaboration is missing between men and women, the enforcement of Hijab on women will continue to be demeaning.

Most books and articles on the subject of Hijab have been written by conscientious women, leaving the majority of men immune from expressing their opinions and taking sides in this battle against half of humanity. If they keep their silence on this issue, it gives the impression that they are insensitive to the suffering of the other half of the population. Men who disagree with the unjust treatment of women by Islamic fundamentalists, but who have chosen to remain silent, must realize that their silence contributes to an increasing number of crimes against women. Male silence further segregates the already divided and tense relationship between Islamic women and men. It is essential for conscientious men to speak up and express their point of view on what amounts to Gendercide.

A small number of younger women, mostly living in the West, have been using Hijab as a means of political uprising against their families and societies, and as a statement against the objectification of women in the West. My purpose is not to downsize their pain. However, I would like to focus on the millions of women who have been forcibly veiled, confined by centuries of tribal, religious, and family customs that tolerate rape and condone murder in the name of Islam. Let us focus on the victimized women for whom Hijab does not represent a choice of modesty, but absolute imprisonment and slavery.

The author of *Women in Islam*, expresses her own objections, with which I agree:

... I for one can not and do not accept the justifications or rationalizations for this current reality. To me, these practices are morally wrong. Just as slavery can not be morally justified today, neither can the contemporary suppression of or discrimination against women be justified. (Speaker-Yuan, 2005)

HISTORICAL POINTS OF VIEWS

After I read Ayatollah Motahari's[1] Farsi book on Hijab, I decided to discuss his point of view. I am saddened to admit that the Ayatollah describes the status of women in Islam at its worst. In his book, he does not hold back from expressing his anger toward women.

---

[1] Ayatollah Morteza Motahari, (February 3, 1920–May 1, 1979) was an Iranian scholar, cleric, University lecturer, and politician.

The Ayatollah cites historical facts about the early days of the Persian Empire, when women had more freedom, but it doesn't seem to improve his opinion of female intelligence. In the days of the early Persian Empire and during the time of Zoroastrianism[1], women benefited from the full respect and admiration of men. They mingled freely among others, women and men alike.

It was during the reign of Darius I[2] (522 BC–486 BC) that their status began to diminish, as wealthy families gradually concealed their women from outside influences. Privileged women appeared in curtained carriages convoyed by household laborers and slaves. Women in those days were especially isolated during their menses. Some form of Hijab then became regularly practiced and appeared before the Persians' acceptance of Islam, some 1350 years ago.

Jawaharlal Nehru, one of India's modern progressive leaders, condemned Hijab as an element to stop women from making progress, which they were accustomed to before the spread of Hijab. Nehru mostly blamed the traditional influences of the Persian and

---

[1] The religious system founded by Zoroaster and set forth in the Avesta, teaching the worship of Ahura Mazda in the context of a universal struggle between the forces of light and of darkness.

[2] Darius I or Darius the Great (Old Persian: Dārayavahuš), (c. 549 BC–486 BC), was a Zoroastrian Persian Shahanshah.

Roman Empires by introducing harems as a means to divide women from men, consequently bringing Hijab. However, when the narrow-minded Ayatollah Motahari expressed his own opinion on the subject, he emphasized that women provided the highest level of pleasure for men. Since social intermingling is bound to bring a disastrous outcome, a physical divider must separate the two sexes from each other.

In pre-Islamic times, without public safety and security, men justified women's imprisonment by admitting that two types of obsessions drove men to commit crimes: other people's wealth and women. However, the Ayatollah states that after the birth of Islam people enjoyed a reasonably safe society, therefore during the rule of Islam, safety could not be the only reason for Hijab's existence.

Honor and Jealousy

The Ayatollah admits that men are obsessed with women's purity, meaning that men want their brides to be virginal and untouched. He admitted that women desire the exact same qualities in their men, however, their intentions differ. According to the Ayatollah, a woman's desire for her husband's purity arises from selfishness and jealousy while a man's intentions are pure and selfless, arising from honor and pride. Supposedly, then, men's feelings are pure and honorable.

Further analyzing the differences between jealousy and honor, he shamelessly concludes that jealousy among women is nothing more than their personal selfishness aroused by ill feeling. A man's honor, on the other hand, is a collective societal feeling benefiting others. According to Motahari, men are Earth's chosen guardians to prevent women's promiscuity. He further compares the male duty of protecting baby-producing women to farmers protecting their seeds and harvests. To him, women are simply breeding machines and baby-producers.

To validate his point of view, Motahari references different *Hadiths* on this subject matter, further emphasizing women's jealousy and men's honor. According to him, women don't want to share their husbands because they are monogamous and want to be the only lover. On the other hand, men don't share the feeling of monogamy except in their duty to prevent their women from bearing another man's child. The Ayatollah confesses that humankind possesses an unlimited appetite for wealth and sex, thus explaining men's infinite desire to seek and conquer all attractive females.

Proving the insanity of his belief system, Motahari grants higher importance to material wealth than to women by indicating that it is man's right to keep his wealth to himself and choose not to share it with others. However, women could become public property, and while one man enjoys her sexually, it must not stop other men from sexually enjoying the same woman (sharing women through *Seegheh*, the Islamic institution of temporary marriage – which amounts to prostitution).

Women's "Deep-Rooted Complex"

This bankrupted belief system leads the Ayatollah to claim that it is a woman's deep-rooted psychological complex towards a man's masculinity and his freedom from monthly menstruation, which causes her to want to stay home and bundle herself up in Hijab. Koranic dictate regards menstruation to be taboo. The Prophet told his followers to consider menstruating women to be physically ill; they could talk to them *[women]*, but they must avoid physical touch.

On other occasions, Motahari describes women as bait, and men as animals, ready to hunt and conquer. He concludes that since women are aware of their physical weakness compared to men, they wittingly use deception to attract them, playing the game of hide and seek.

Despite the Ayatollah's misogynistic sentiments, even he had to admit that the Koran does not have a verse dedicated to Hijab except when referring to the Prophet's wives, requiring them to dress modestly in public and act as exemplary women. The Koran, on two occasions *[Suras: Nour and Ahzaab]*, reminds women to be physically and socially modest while in the company of men and forbids women from drawing attention to themselves through playful attributes such as their voice and body language. Moreover, women are not allowed to show any skin except the backs of their hands. In some Islamic societies, women are allowed to show their whole face or only their eyes.

Motahari reminds his readers that men study harder and conduct business better when women are plain to look at. What he really means is for women to cover their hair and wear baggy, unattractive clothes in order to prevent men from exposure to unnecessary distractions. According to the Ayatollah and millions of other Islamic men around the world, the women's feelings about all this are not a concern.

He believes that men are the superior gender, physically, and mentally. Women, on the other hand, only excel at feelings and emotions. He concludes that in order for women to gain respect, they must stay modest, humble, and reserved.

The Ayatollah, does however, give women the responsibility of not only to wear Hijab, but also to believe in it whole-heartedly as if their sole obligation in life is to prevent men from committing evil acts of temptation. He says that *Allah* gave women the obligation of maintaining integrity and chastity at all costs. Despite referring to Islamic laws supporting women's freedom, Motahari emphasizes two Koranic rules: First, women must not appear outside of their homes unless they follow the rules of Hijab, and second, that women must not leave their homes unless they have the full consent of their husbands prior to each departure.

Disregarding the societal contributions of millions of Iranian women before the Islamic Revolution, the Ayatollah calls their work purposeless, performed only to accumulate wealth while destroying core family values. In his opinion, the only truly productive women are either among the respectable fundamentalist families or in villages among the peasants.

My daughter, expressed her feelings after reading this section:

It makes me very sad for those parts of culture and humanity that are deeply lost and must feel a desperate sadness and loneliness because they do not enjoy the joys of femininity, such as color, beauty, singing, dancing, and all the things that are part of the uniquely feminine spirit. All those things being hidden under dark, drab cloth...and why? Then nobody in the society gets to enjoy these free, wonderful pleasures of life! So strange that anyone (the men in ruling positions of Islam) would want to repress their own joy so much!

Ayatollah Khomeini's[1] writings, speeches and Q & A sessions have been compiled by The Institute for Compilation and Publication of Imam Khomeini's Works - International Affairs Division, with hundreds of pages, devoted to the subject of Islamic women.

---

[1] Ayatollah Khomeini – (24 September 1902 – 3 June 1989) an Iranian religious leader and politician, and leader of the 1979 Iranian Revolution which saw the overthrow of Mohammad Reza Pahlavi, the Shah of Iran. Following the revolution and a national referendum, Khomeini became the country's Supreme Leader—a position created in the constitution as the highest ranking political and religious authority of the nation.

Khomeini blamed the Pahlavi Dynasty for corrupting women. Before entering Iran in early 1979, he was asked about the fate of Iranian women and their fear of being sent socially backwards, to the time before the Shah's progressive plans on freedom for women. The Ayatollah proclaimed *"... Islam not only sanctions freedom for women, it is actually the founder of freedom for women in all the dimensions which exist for a woman."*

On one hand, he speaks of men and women as equals in the eyes of God and Islam when he says:

Islam grants women a say in all affairs, just as it grants men a say. Just as men should avoid corruption, so too should women. Women should not allow themselves to be playthings in the hands of dissolute youths, they should not lower their station and, God forbid, come out into the streets dressed up and made up, placing themselves in full view of depraved men. Women must act like true human beings; they must be pious. Women enjoy a dignified position; they have free will, just as men have. God created you free and gave you dignity.

Having said this, he then ordered women to obey their husbands and seek their permission on daily conduct when he says: *"... but they must obey their husbands in marital affairs. They should not leave their homes without their husbands' consent."*

Television & Film

On the topic of alcohol and film in women's lives, Khomeini states:

... women in their role as human beings can work alongside men to establish the Islamic society, but not if they wish to act as mere objects. Women do not have the right to lower themselves to such a level, nor do men have the right to think of them as such. As to those things known as entertainment, Islam opposes anything that tends to lead human beings towards acquiring a frivolous nature or towards self-estrangement. The consumption of alcohol is forbidden in Islam, as are films, which pervert the exalted nature of the human being.

When asked for permission to watch films on TV, which included unveiled women and music, he responded:

There is no problem concerning the viewing of foreign films in which the actresses are not known and which do not have a corrupt influence. Dance music is forbidden, but there is no problem with other types of music.

Answers Fallaci's Question

In a 1979 interview with Oriana Fallaci[1], Ayatollah Khomeini answered a question about whether it is fair and right for

women who helped with the Iranian revolution to hide themselves away and cover up under *chador*. Khomeini responded:

First of all, this is something that is their [Iranian women] choice, and they have chosen it for themselves. What right do you have to deprive them of their choice? If we tell the people to come out and demonstrate their approval for the Islamic dress, whether the chador or some other form, out of our population of 35 million [population of Iran in 1979], 33 million would

---

[1] Oriana Fallaci (29 June 1929 – 15 September 2006) was an Italian journalist, author, and political interviewer. A former partisan during World War II, she had a long and successful journalistic career.

come out. What right do you have to stop them? What kind of dictatorship is this you want to impose on the women? Secondly, we do not say a woman has to wear a specific type of dress, particularly in the case of women your age there are no specifications [Oriana was approximately 50 years old during the interview]. We are concerned mainly with the younger women who when they make up and dress up, draw hordes of young men after them. It is these women we are stopping. They don't need your sympathy.

It is widely known that Ms. Fallaci ripped off her headscarf after Khomeini's comment to her and Khomeini aborted the interview session and left the room.

Describing Women

During the Pahlavi Regime

The Ayatollah's anger becomes clear when he describes the status of women during the Shah's regime and calls women to repent:

Women are creatures who can destroy a power that seems everlasting, a demonic power. During their reigns, Riza Khan [sic] and Mohammad Riza Khan vulgarized women, dragging them down from that status they once enjoyed, … He continues: Women during the time of Riza Khan and Mohammad Riza Pahlavi were oppressed creatures and did not know it. It is doubtful that women were subjected to as much oppression during the Age of Ignorance [pre-Islamic era] as they were during the reigns of these two men, or as much degradation.

And he ultimately calls upon women and invites them to embrace [his] Islam:

Oh honorable women, awaken! Be alert; do not let yourself be deceived by those devils who wish to pull you into this maelstrom. They are alluring and deceitful; they are out to cheat you just as the cursed Shah was. Take refuge in Islam. Islam will bring you happiness. (Imam Khomeini's Works, 2001)

Married Women

Ayatollah Khomeini's instructions forbid married women to leave their houses without their husbands' permission. These instructions are not to protect women, but only to maintain pleasure for men.

Here is the essence of his dictate as described *Resaleh*, a book of his teachings:

She must remain at his disposal for the fulfillment of any one of his desires, and may not refuse herself to him except for a religiously valid reason. If she is very submissive to him, the husband must provide her with her food, clothing, and lodging, whether or not he has the means to do so. A woman who refuses herself to her husband is guilty, and may not demand from him food, clothing, lodging or any later sexual relations; however, she retains the right to be paid damages if she is repudiated. (Resaleh Khomeini)

In Khomeini's Islam, men and women clearly do not share any kind of equal partnership, but rather a businesslike relation, where a woman who does not properly serve her man can be discarded, like a cow that no longer produces milk. This is not only an insult to Islamic women, but also to Islamic men, as they are missing true communication and companionship in their lives.

At a 1968 seminar studying Hijab held by the Islamic Republic of Iran and attended by members of the Iranian Parliament and the

Tehran Department of Education, Dr. Zahra Rahnavard, author of *Beauty of Concealment and Concealment of Beauty*, drew the resemblance between a garden, fruit, and the beauty of Hijab. It was a hopeless endeavor to attract intelligent women to her way of thinking. It is unclear to me whether she is describing the different forms of Hijab or trying to whet men's appetites as she compares women and Hijab to delectable varieties of fruit:

Hijab is like a scenery, a panorama or a garden, a garden full of fruits of different colours. You can select any one of the thousands of rooms with thousands of windows, and from its frame look at the garden, stretch your hand and pick off a fruit. You can pick off the entire garden at one and the same time like a single fruit, satisfy with its flavour your heart and soul, and make the garden, the Hijab, a solace for your (disturbed) inner self. Of all the myriad windows through which one can look into the garden, let us have a look at Hijab through the window of beauty, a deep window, a window made of the wood of Sidra (the Lote Tree in the Seventh Heaven) with the scent of eternal memories, a latticed window with variegated glass, illumining your soul with multicolour lustre, a window of beauty of age-long human civilization, a window of centuries old human presence on the earth, or even older, a window dating back to the very age of creation or existence itself, a window of beauty!

(http://www.al-islam.org/beautyofconcealment/)

"Old Praying Woman in Jamé Mosque" by Hamed Saber

(Distributed under the Creative Commons 3.0 License)

In her speech she further explains that, except for the less than one percent of women in Iranian society who were mesmerized and influenced by the evil Imperialism of the former Pahlavi regime the rest are *"noble, modest, and peerless."* Interestingly, she envisions women adjusting easily to the political rulings of any particular society.

Rahnavard symbolizes all developments throughout women's lives as curtains drawn on them. For example, the: *"curtain of shape, curtain of status, curtain of class, curtain of reputation, and curtain of respectability."* In my opinion, this analogy is distressing as well as fascinating. Instead of describing those developments as windows of opportunity, which open up to women at different cycles in their lives, she compares them to curtains to further cover, compartmentalize, and confine women.

In an opportunistic attempt, Dr. Zahra creates a powerful image of women only to blame them for the so-called Imperialist attacks on Islamic regions. She scolds women for their ignorance by inviting the Imperialists into their lives. She proclaims that the so-called evil Imperialistic West preys upon misguided women and uses them as instruments for delivering destruction into the Islamic cultures.

IS HIJAB GOOD OR BAD?

We have already established that Hijab comes in a variety of forms, depending on the local ruling class. For example, as mentioned in the introduction, Reza Shah unveiled Iranian women during his governance and imposed European dress on

men and women. He made positive steps such as making sure women enter schools and the work force. However, his abrupt measures to *forcibly abolishing* the wearing of the veil by 1936, created ill feelings among religious hardliners as well as traditional women. Change did not take place through comprehensive education of the public. My point is that we must be conscious of propaganda. At different times in history, the ruling class, religious or non-religious, has made decisions over women's lives to support their own agendas, and that alone proves that Hijab is not universal and timeless. Rather, it is another type of uniform imposed upon women by men, to serve their current cultural, political, and environmental needs.

I wish for young women in Western societies, those who have decided to wear Hijab, to recognize the fact that living in a democratic society allows them their freedom of choice. I also beg of them to remember the millions of women living in fascistic and dictatorial societies, forced to wear Hijab without having any other options. To the women who believe that Hijab provides them with an identity, I ask them to think of the millions of faceless Muslim women in the *burqa* and similar coverings who are fighting to claim their identity by burning themselves alive.

I have heard women justify Hijab as a way to be sure that men judge them not by their appearance but by their personality, character, and morals. My question to those women is why they are so profoundly concerned about men's evaluation of their characters. Aren't right actions enough? Why must a particular appearance assure women's decency and purity as well? Should it even matter what men think of women? Who are men to judge women, especially after reading the Koran, *Hadiths*, Khomeini's *Resaleh*, and other writings that expose the one-track, sexually obsessed minds of some Islamic men?

Muslim women must find the perfect religious solution by looking within themselves. There, they will find answers or look for an alternate faith with a more commonsense approach to issues in relation to humanity as whole. Numerous soul-searching women have looked for the root cause of the need to cover up, and have arrived at the same conclusion as Saleemah, the author of *Living Islam Outloud*:

I began to reevaluate my life and, especially, the rituals I performed. I decided to stop doing things that didn't make sense to me, so I stopped wearing Hijab – not because I felt oppressed wearing it, but rather because I realized that I had never chosen Hijab for myself. (Abdul-Ghafur, 2005)

She continues to explain that as she gained more knowledge and understanding of the Koran and its companion books, she realized that exteriors do not explain women's position in religion or society. Therefore, she had created her own incarceration and captivity.

Let us ponder the following story told by Samina Ali in *Living Islam Outloud*. Samina described that every morning, her mother warned her about the consequences of interacting with men outside her immediate family. Her mother kept whispering in Samina's ear that if she engaged in any type of sexual activity: *"He will know."* According to Samina, her mother was referring to *"my future husband, the one my parents would choose for me."* Samina kept asking her mother how her future husband would know? And her mother would answer; *"He just will. When a valuable vase has even the faintest crack in it, it's useless. Don't become useless, Samina."* Samina explains that she started to compare men to God since they seemed to know everything.

Once I did [associate men with God], I began to be conscious of how men's superiority over women was tightly woven into our parent's teachings of Islam… therefore, my girlfriends and I grew up believing that we were priceless vases that could easily shatter, thus shattering our family's reputation. We were to believe this would happen simply because we were women and acts of self-control were beyond us… (Abdul-Ghafur, 2005)

Might it not be better for us women to concentrate on ourselves and how we perceive each other?

International Women's Day demonstrators shortly after the

Islamic Revolution, Tehran, Iran, March 8, 1979.
(Iranian.com/History/2000/March/Women/demo24.html)

WHO IS TO GAIN?

WHAT ARE THE INTENTIONS?

The collective antiquated minds of elders and traditionalists in Muslim societies have led us into a tangled web of insults and limitations imposed on women from the minute they are born into

women as objects, born to serve in kitchens and bedrooms. Women prefer to deliver male children and understand that they, as females, will not have much influence in their children's lives. They must live by the fact that decision-making belongs to men in the family. It takes a collective effort and societal initiative to help these disempowered women begin to heal. We must acknowledge the injustice and wrongdoings of centuries old traditions, and then learn how to eliminate those contentious situations.

A new generation of Muslim men and women must open their hearts to feel the deep-rooted pain and suffering. They must shoulder the responsibility and face the problem head on, demanding that the *mullahs* explain their twisted and dark intentions against half of the Earth's population. Whether we are referring to verses of the holy Koran or rulings initiated by charlatans with horrific self-centered intentions, the outcome is the same; the ruination of fragile baby girls destined to eternal suffering: No more. It is time to claim our consciousness and stand up for humanity.

United Nations Chief Ban Ki-Moon encourages men to end violence against women: *"Break the silence, when you witness violence against women and girls, do not sit back. Act. Advocate. Unite to change the practices and attitudes that incite, perpetrate and condone this violence."*

He equally condemns violence against women at the hands of their husbands or intimate partners and encourages men to raise awareness that women also belong in schools and workplaces, and are not simply limited to the home or the fields. South African Nobel Peace Laureate, Archbishop Desmond Tutu, said: *"You are a weak man if you use your physical superiority to assault and brutalize women."*

I am mystified by the amount of male anger directed toward women in the Islamic teachings. Islam forbids women to appear in public or speak to non-related men and discourages men and women from creating a healthy atmosphere filled with the communication and an exchange of ideas. On the contrary, Islam encourages gender segregation by planting seeds of disrespect, inequality, and distrust.

Whether it is true or false, Islam accuses men and women of having only sexual intention for meeting in public and wanting to communicate, and that it will end in some sort of sexual misdeed. Islam's solution is for women to cover their hair and body and not raise their voice in public. Actually, Islamic fundamentalists prefer women not to appear in public in the first place, but to spend their lives in the four corners of their fathers' and husbands' kitchens and bedrooms!

Ayatollah Motahari, in his book about Hijab, expressed his opinion by telling the following story: during a hot summer day in Medina[1], one of the Prophet Mohammad's followers noticed an attractive woman walking on the street. She was wearing her headscarf according to the current time's custom, which allowed her neck and cleavage to be visible. The man, hypnotized by her beauty, started following her without paying attention to the road ahead. Soon after, he bumped into a sharp object protruding from the wall and injured his head. Angered by this incident, with his hand to his bleeding head, he went to see the Prophet and complained about the beautiful woman who dared to display her beauty, causing him to

---

[1] Medina; officially *al-Madinah al-Munawwarah*) is a city in the Hejaz region of western Saudi Arabia, and serves as the capital of the Al Madinah Province. It is the second holiest city in Islam, and the burial place of the Prophet Muhammad and his home after the *Hijrah*.

have an accident. Miraculously, a Koranic verse arrived from an angel, proclaiming that women must wear head coverings not only to hide their hair, but their cleavage as well, and cover every other inch of visible flesh.

... they should not display their beauty and ornaments except what appear thereof; that they should draw veils over their bosoms and not display their beauty except to their husbands, their fathers, their husbands' fathers, their sons... (An-Nur 24:31)

It seems the logical advice to the man would be to pay more attention to the road, and lower his own lustful gaze!

How is it that a woman's hair and voice has so much power over Muslim men, which non-Muslim men are immune from? How is it that non-Muslim men are able to control themselves in the company of women, while Muslim men seem to respond only as lusty animals? What has been outlined in *Allah's* diverse plan, that is only in Muslim women's best interest, and not women in other religions? Muslim men can look at non-Muslim women, and no one is struck by lightning.

Life goes on when millions of Muslim men travel abroad and interact with women. Nevertheless, they go home to their veiled wives. Does it mean they are battling their sexual demons all day long? Are they on the verge of losing control of themselves while they are outside of their homes? Or is it simply another conspiracy cooked up by the Islamic clergy to keep women under wraps, away from hustle and bustle of the world.

I always thought this was one excuse for men to avoid the challenges associated with improving their behavior or communication skills with their spouses.

At home, they can simply shut women out from their thoughts, important business affairs, family decisions or any other discussions typically requiring the involvement of both partners.

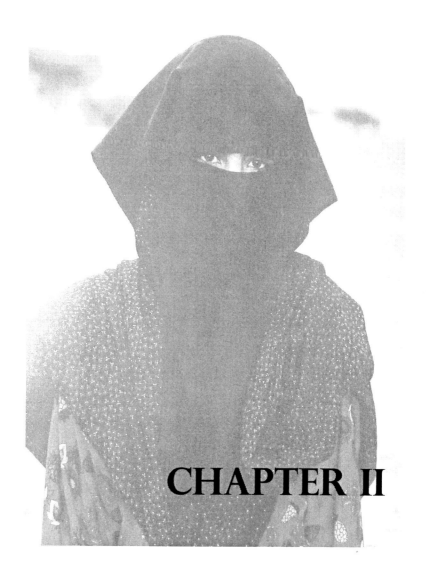

CHAPTER II

CULTURE & CUSTOM

"In any moment of decision, the best thing you can do is the right thing, the next best thing is the wrong thing, and the worst thing you can do is nothing."

Theodore Roosevelt

WOMEN'S OBEDIENCE

Millions of women have been brought up to believe that it is both a woman's fate and the will of *Allah* to live under the authority of men. The Koran elucidates the will of *Allah* when speaking to men about punishing disloyal women by refusing to provide them with food, or beating them to different degrees, depending on the punishment required. Women are forgiven only after they become obedient. Different clerics have found explanations more appealing to their appetite, such as the ridiculous and comical *Hadiths*: *"The woman who dies and with whom the husband is satisfied will go to Paradise."* Or: *"A wife should never refuse herself to her husband even if they are on the saddle of a camel." (Islam-watch.org/IbnWarraq/Islam's-Shame-Veil-Tears.htm)*

Studies on women in Islamic nations revealed a widespread fear of *Allah's* punishment and hellfire for not wearing Hijab as a symbol of modesty and chastity. According to the Koran:

She must be well covered, including her face, to avoid tempting any men who might be around; she must move with her head bowed down looking neither left nor right... She must not walk in the middle of the road among men. The Prophet, on noticing the confusion upon leaving a mosque said: "You women do not have the right to walk amongst men – stick to the sides"... She must walk in a chaste and modest manner (24:31). When talking to stranger, her voice must remain normal (33:32).

Since women are known as the peacemakers in their families, they are further coerced to remain voiceless in order to maintain harmony. Men's treatment of women can be compared to a game of ping-pong, with the women being tossed back and forth from one man's dominance to another (father to husband and back to father again, in cases of divorce).

Unfortunately, most popular advice given to women comes from men. An Islamic philosopher, al-Ghazali[1], steered women's attention to only the following:

Her sole worry should be her virtue, her home, as well as her prayers and her fast... She should accept what her husband gives her as sufficient sexual needs at any moment... She should be clean and ready to satisfy her husband's sexual needs at any moment. (Hurley, 2001)

Some of these backwards customs and practices can be found among the four volumes of the Ayatollah Khomeini's *Resaleh* teachings. For example, men, in the *Tahrirolvasyleh* (1990), receive instructions on how to kill a variety of domestic animals after they

---

[1] Abu Hamid *al-Ghazali* (450 – 505 AH/1058 – 1111 AD), philosopher and mystic.

have had sexual intercourse with them. In the original Farsi edition of *Resaleh*, in Problems 2631-2632, the Ayatollah referred to the mule, ass, cow, camel, and sheep among the animals that men may engage in sexual intercourse. Khomeini then reminds men that after committing bestiality, they should not consider selling the *"traumatized"* animal's meat.

As described in the book's fourth edition, men are allowed to seek sexual enjoyment from girls as early as infancy, as long as it is not through the vagina. If damage occurs due to excessive penetration, the man is responsible for the girl's wellbeing, but is not required to marry her. The Ayatollah states that it is better for the girl to marry and leave her father's home before her menses has begun, and for fathers who successfully marry their daughters off at such early age, an eternal place in heaven is promised.

Permanent and Temporary Marriage

Islam's proclamation that women are unable to survive without men's financial and physical support allows fundamentalists to impose polygamy as a means for men to have multiple wives. Islamic laws allow men to have four simultaneous wives, *"marry of the women, who seem good to you, two, three, or four ," (Koran 4:3)* and temporarily marry as many times as they can afford, physically and financially. These temporary marriages of convenience have been designed to accommodate men's sexual relations outside of their permanent marriages. Iranians call it *Seegheh* and this temporary marriage, condoned in Khomeini's *Resaleh,* can last as long as an hour, a day, a month, a year or longer.

The *Seegheh* contract does not require additional witnesses and the men are only obligated to feed the contracted woman for the duration. If the woman becomes pregnant during the period of *Seegheh*, the child belongs to the husband, unless he refuses to keep the offspring. In order to monitor potential pregnancy, women are allowed to enter a new contract only every forty-five days. However, the sole purpose of *Seegheh* is men's sexual enjoyment and not the production of babies. Women are merely a rental property. *Seegheh*, known in Arabic as *Mut'a*, originated in an ancient nomadic culture of the Arabian Peninsula and was adapted by Islam. *Mut'a*, in Arabic, means 'joy.'

Ayatollah Khomeini's verdict on temporary marriage, which amounts to prostitution, is: *"It is permissible to do Mut'a with an adulteress, but with aversion, particularly if she is a well-known prostitute. If Mut'a is done with her, she should be told to give-up her profession."*

In his book, *Women and the Koran,* Anwar Hekmat disapproves of Islam's rationale for adopting polygamy during early Islamic battles as a means to shelter and feed the excess women after the men had died. We can examine it by reviewing other cultures with similar situations and their way of solving this problem. Devastated nations such as Germany, Russia, and Japan, even after multiple wars, did not introduce the institution of polygamy as their solution to cope with the increased number of single women in their societies.

Another Islamic reason for introducing polygamy is to prevent prostitution, which again shows Islam's lack of regard for women by considering them helpless objects of pleasure. Hekmat further exclaims; *"this ridiculous argument strips women of their intelligence, dignity, and wisdom to choose millions of other occupations available to women today."* *(1997)*

The truth behind the polygamous urge may be found in this telling quote from Islamic philosopher al-Ghazali:

Some men have such a compelling sexual desire that one woman is not sufficient to protect them (from adultery). Such men, therefore, preferably marry more than one woman and may have up to four wives. (Ihy'a Uloum ed-Din by Ghazali, Vol. 2, Kitab Adab Al-Nikah, p. 34) *(http://www.arabicbible.com/christian/Women_in_Islam.htm)*

A wife's role is made clear by Ayatollah Khomeini in Problem 2412 of *Resaleh*, in which he commands married women not to leave their houses without their husbands' full permission, even insisting, in Problem 894, that women perform their daily prayers only inside the home, preferably in the confines of a closet. Furthermore, he instructs women to be available and ready to please their husbands, upon request. It is only after a married woman fulfills her conjugal duty that a husband is required to provide her with food, clothing, and shelter. In Problem 2413, he forbids men to feed, clothe, and shelter disobedient women, who are considered guilty.

There are austere rules about the importance of a girls' virginity on her wedding night. In Problem 2444, Khomeini permits husbands to immediately annul the marriage on the wedding night if he discovers his bride is not a virgin.

Deep Rooted Anger Against Women

During the 1979 Iranian Islamic Revolution, the most common slogan shouted at women was, *"wear your scarf or be whacked on your head."* These men were representing religious leaders and supposedly the champions of human rights carrying the torch of change from the Shah's brutality and injustice. Who were they fooling? They didn't even try to tone it down and win women's hearts and votes. To these men, women were, and continue to be, nothing but objects, and they weren't ashamed to admit it. These types of slogans and men's attitudes toward women are not random coincidences, but deep-rooted cultural dispositions.

For centuries, men have exploited women to satisfy their physical pleasures, utilized them for comfort during their senseless battles, used them as gift offerings to close business deals and sentenced them to torture and death without cause, in order to expel their internal anger and vengeance.

In fact, as cited in the book, *Jimmy Carter: The Liberal Left & World Chaos*, when *LaMonde's*[1] reporter Paul Balta interviewed Khomeini in January of 1979 as he *[Khomeini]* was getting ready to leave exile, and make his way back to Iran. He questioned Khomeini about the status of Iranian women under Khomeini's regime. The Ayatollah's answer from his temporary suburban residence in Paris was; *"Our women fight like lions. They deserve our admiration. In the Islamic State, they will have the status that they deserve."* A few weeks later,

---

[1] *LaMonde* Magazine - A French newspaper

witnessed by the world, the Ayatollah, accompanied by hundreds of reporters including Balta, flew to Tehran on a chartered Air France jet. In the blink of an eye, *"Khomeini returned the women of Iran to the Dark Ages."* Balta further explains:

Khomeini outlined the main orientations of the future Islamic Republic and proclaimed compulsory wearing of the chador – "veil" – which had been abolished by the Shah. At the conclusion of the ceremony [in Qum], I expressed my surprise about the chador, but he replied to me; "I told you they deserve our admiration. It is always the case, but I added that in the Islamic State, they will have the status that they deserve." (Evans, 2009)

During the Pahlavi Dynasty, women in Iran had reasonable freedom, but during the Islamic Republics' ruling, women were stripped of all of their freedom and taken back fourteen centuries. In the last thirty years, the struggle and sacrifice of millions of courageous women forced the government to give back some limited freedoms. However, due to the influence of religious fanaticism in people's lives, the progress has been slow and tedious.

For decades, Iranian fanatics have attacked and labeled everyone who supports women's rights as lovers of the Western imperialists and supporters of prostitution. The Islamic Republic of Iran's clerics have labeled educated and outspoken women as Westernized dolls and empty-headed puppets of corrupt Western culture. They immediately mythologized the Prophet's daughter as an exemplary Islamic woman; a true images of modesty, obedience, and purity. The Islamic fanatics' idea of a pure woman is an imitation of a 1400-year-old myth and symbol. But even in the Prophet's time, senseless violence towards women was justified.

...(Umar) found the Prophet sitting sad and silent with his wives around him...(Umar) decided to say something which would make the Prophet laugh, so he said, "Messenger of God, I wish you had seen the daughter of Kharija when she asked me for extra money and I got up and slapped her on the neck." God's messenger laughed and said, "They are around me as you see asking for extra money." Abu Bakr then got up, went to A'isha and slapped her on the neck, and Umar did the same to Hafsa. (Mishkat Al-Masabih: volume 2, p. 690; Muslim: book 9, number 3506, Siddiqui).

(http://www.answering-islam.org/Green/womenstatus.htm)

From the beginning of the Iranian Islamic Revolution, opposition groups joined forces on one subject: women. They used the same old tactics as their pre-Islamic ancestors to denigrate women to the pathetic level of tools, objects and instruments spreading seeds of conspiracy and destruction among people. Stories of old Islamic wars show captors mocking their war prisoners in public by forcing them to knit and weave with the tools that women used, which was considered one of the worst humiliations for men.

In her book *The Caged Virgin*, Ayaan Hirsi Ali explains that in exploitative and backwards societies, men and boys don't receive the benefit of a well-balanced upbringing and are usually raised by uneducated and deprived mothers. In the absence of exemplary females as role models, young boys grow up behaving awkwardly around women, which in fact positions men at a disadvantage, socially and developmentally. Due to the *"disproportionately strong emphasis on 'manliness'"* in Islamic societies, there is great disequilibrium between the sexes.

Hirsi Ali recalled a childhood memory of her aunt putting a piece of meat out in the sun, which drew a cluster of ants and flies. She then compared men to these creatures, saying: *"When they see a woman, they can't restrain their lust."*

In Saudi Arabia, women must become faceless and anonymous in order to remain safe. In *Lifting the Veil*, the author asks:

How is it that a formless, seamless, colorless garment is required in order for a woman to be considered decent and respectable? ... Are Saudi men so brutal, so aggressive that the women need to retreat into multiple yards of stifling hot cloth in order to be protected? (Parshall, 2002)

If a woman must cover her hair, face, and body to defend her honor from men, then women have abided by men's wishes, putting themselves in an inferior position. Arab men in pre-Islamic societies used to bury their infant girls alive and today Islamic men, Arab and non-Arab alike, stone their daughters, wives and mothers to death, justifying their senseless acts as honor or chastity killing.

Women have been beaten into the idea of admiring masculinity and its roughness as a superior quality. Men on the other hand, have learned to consider feminine qualities as inferior, fragile, and too tender. What has become a common thread between the Islamic nations is the general populations' high level of poverty, deprivation, and lack of non-Koranic education. What are also missing from many Islamic societies are basic freedoms and a lack of women's rights. Individuals, particularly women, are in a tremendous struggle to maintain their basic civil liberties. These debilitating situations occur in most, if not all, of the Islamic countries and are proof of patriarchal culture at its worst.

We must ask these key and vital questions: what is the root cause of men's fear of women; and if women unite and decide to unveil, what is it that men fear the most?

LIMITATIONS PLACED ON WOMEN

Women and Sports

It is important to consider the necessity of physical activity and most Muslim women's lack of participation in this key developmental area. Muslim girls are discouraged from simple activities such as running, jumping, climbing trees, and rock climbing. I grew up hearing the myth that too much running, jumping, biking or swimming, especially while menstruating, is not healthy for girls and that it would cause lasting damage to the reproductive area. I never understood whether they were genuinely concerned about a girl's health or afraid that she might lose her chance to produce babies.

In today's Iran and in many other Islamic countries, most women are not allowed to participate or be present in public areas to watch sports. Iranian women who have dared to form biking groups have run into hostile crowds of men, which in some cases had to be pushed back by local police or the military.

Photo:Masood Sheikh Veisi   FARS NEWS AGENCY

http://www.skyscrapercity.com

A dour and restricted reality for women shrouded in Hijab. (Fotolia.com)

Women and the Arts

Women's limited participation does not end with sports. Some areas of art and entertainment, such as cinema, theatre, painting, sculpture, and calligraphy are among the activities that women have been denied access. Women's participation in any type of group or individual singing and dancing events has also been prohibited. After the Islamic Revolution, most entertainers and artists fled the country, seeking refuge elsewhere. The Islamic film trade has been dominated by men with a primarily men's point of view. More and more, women are making their presence known in the cinema industry introducing Islamic and men-women issues. However, countries like Saudi Arabia still prohibit women from going to cinema.

Women and Education

In most Islamic countries, it is customary for boys to benefit from more education than girls. Families rarely pay the same attention to their daughters' level of education, and this neglect is intensified in rural areas. Girls are simply their mothers' helpers in the kitchen and around the house until it is time for them to become someone's wife and perform the same duties in another setting. Since daughters grow up to become other families' properties, it has been considered unnecessary to spend time and money on their education. Boys, on the other hand, are considered the extended arms of their fathers and their prosperity benefits not only their own family, but their parents as well.

In some societies, it is customary for most urban and rural families to end their daughters' education after completing the first few years and concentrate on grooming them to become skilled future wives by learning domestic talents such as cooking and sewing. Girls in rural areas hold additional domestic duties such as weaving, taking care of the animals and cattle, washing and preparing wool, and harvesting. There is a saying that *"too much education will open a girl's eyes and ears"* and the narrow-minded men of those families are clueless on how to deal with it. Sadly, the decision that they all arrive at is to repress women further.

Women and the Wedding Night

There are numerous stories about girls as young as nine years old being removed from their classrooms and brought home to be prepared for their weddings. Let us not forget that the majority of these girls have not had any exposure to basic sex education, and some of them have not even started their menstrual period, which means they don't have any idea what to expect on their wedding nights. Their first sexual encounter becomes a nightmare, sometimes with a husband as old as their father or grandfather.

Occasionally, poor rural families sell their daughters to older and wealthier men for money. This centuries' old practice also takes place among tribal families for monetary or political reasons. Exchanging brides is one way to settle fights and bad blood between tribal families.

It is customary for most fathers to choose a suitable groom according to their family's social status, decide on a dowry, shake hands, bless the occasion, and set up a wedding date that fits their social calendar. Women in the family, including the mother of the bride, learn about the upcoming event after everything has been settled among the men.

Young brides – a miserable life for little girls in Saudi Arabia. Photo by Pooja, December 22, 2008. (Themuslimwoman.org)

The humiliation for these wretched girls does not end there. On the wedding night, elders of both families wait for a bloody cloth to be handed to them by the groom. This bloody cloth, displayed to the families of the newlyweds, is evidence of the conquest of his virginal bride. Only then can the family call it a successful match. In short, sometimes the entire family arranges and approves of a young virgin's rape by her new husband.

Hirsi Ali speaks of Somali girls who have been stitched up after their circumcision. Their mantra while growing up is *"just keep your stitches intact."* These girls know full well that *"in the case of a new husband discovering a disturbance in her stitches, the new bride suddenly becomes a whore."*

My Grandmother's Story

My paternal grandmother, small stature with a candid sense of humor, learned to wear chador as part of her Islamic and family tradition. She used to tell us her wedding story. At age twelve or thirteen she was snatched by her mother and aunts from the back room where she and her sisters were playing with dolls. They dressed her up and took her to another room that was beautifully decorated and carpeted. On the floor, a Koran was placed on a silver tray along with some sweets delicacies in silver dishes. They made her sit on the floor in front of the decorations, which included a three-foot tall standing mirror with matching candleholders on each side. She was crying and pleading with her mother and aunts, wondering what would happen next. After all, she had heard stories from the married women in her family of the similar matrimonial conditions they had been forced to accept.

My grandmother used to puff on her cigarette at this time, her eyes distant, and continue with her story: "The women left me in the room without showing remorse, except whispering to me that they had done the same thing and that this would not be the death of me. If they survived the ordeal, so would I. They wanted me to put my trust in their hands, since it could be far worse."

My grandmother waited for what seemed like an eternity when the door finally opened and an old man walked in. She held her breath for the longest time and thought to herself that he, the old man, was to be her husband until death took her away to freedom. To her disbelief, he came in, kissed her on her forehead, put a piece of jewelry in her shivering palm, and left the room. At this moment, we, her grandchildren, giggled and laughed to make my grandmother laugh with us.

Puffing on her cigarette again, she would continue, knowing that we were dying to know who the older man was. At that moment, she did not know who he was, still under the impression that the old man was going to be her husband and that the ceremony was over. Only later, the door opened again and this time a young, handsome man walked in and sat next to her. I cannot remember if they exchanged words and if she told us what they said to each other. All I remember is that my cousins and I would cheer and tease my grandmother, telling her she found a good catch: my handsome and powerful grandfather.

My grandmother died in her early sixties of heart disease. She went through fourteen pregnancies, losing six of her children to different childhood diseases common in the 1920's and 30's, and managed to raise eight of them. I would give a few years of my life for a chance to sit with her and ask if she also thought he was handsome and if she enjoyed her life with such a powerful man who spent so little time with her except when he impregnated her, repeatedly.

She died, while in her favorite religious city far away from her hometown, among her friends and her favorite saint's tomb. It almost was by design, just the way she wanted it to be. Her faith and purity prevailed and in the end, she got her wish: to not be buried in the family mausoleum, next to her husband and his family.

TRIBAL PRACTICES

Honor Killing

Honor killing is a tribal behavior that can be traced to pre-Islamic culture. The survival of family honor justifies the killing of women and girls accused of adultery, which, in this case, does not necessarily mean sexual relation of any kind. Often, talking to a man outside of immediate family is evidence enough for conviction.

The killing takes place when and how the offended man decides to commit the ordeal. He decides what weapon to use and when to perform the act, and oftentimes the man is praised and his family is satisfied that their honor has been returned:

Men are in charge of women, because Allah hath made the one of them to excess the other, and because they spend of their property. Good women are obedient, guarding in secret that which Allah hath guarded. As for those from whom ye fear rebellion, admonish them and banish them and scourge them. (Koran, 4:34)

Honor killing can be traced back to Hammurabi[1] and Assyrian[2] laws from 1200 B.C., as a woman's chastity was considered her family's property. In most conformist societies, conversation between unrelated women and men may be considered adultery, and is

---

[1] Hammurabi, King of Babylonia, and the greatest ruler in the first Babylonian dynasty. Although he was a successful military leader and administrator, Hammurabi is primarily remembered for his codification of the laws governing Babylonian life, known as the Code of Hammurabi.

[2] Assyria in earliest historical times referred to a region on the Upper Tigris River, named for its original capital, the ancient city of Ashur.

therefore punishable by death at the hands of a woman's immediate male family member. In some cases, it only takes a rumor of wrongdoing to ignite the flame.

In March of 2000, UNICEF Executive Director Carol Bellamy took a strong position against cultural injustice aimed at innocent women and girls around the world. She specifically mentioned such brutal acts as *honor killing, acid violence[1], female infanticide, and bride burning[2]* at the hands of male family members. She blamed those societies for admiring the perpetrators for their violent acts and encouraged governments and conscientious groups to become involved in preventing the continued crimes committed against women and girls.

---

[1] Perpetrators of these attacks throw acid at their victims (usually at their faces), burning them, and damaging skin tissue.

[2] Bride burning is when husbands are unsatisfied with their wives' dowry, among other reasons, and decide to cause a domestic accident *[kitchen stove catching fire]*, thus burning their wives.

Crimes of Honour, Shelley Saywell's film documenting the stories of

three women in Jordan and Israel's West Bank.

(Themuslimwoman.org)

Recent reports from Basra, Iraq indicate that religious extremism targets women and that those men are getting away with murder.

Their [women's] mutilated bodies are dumped on the streets or in garbage dumps with notes attached to them accusing them of adultery and other 'honor crimes', thereby justifying their hideous crime of killing these women. (Sept 8 2008, themuslimwoman.org)

In *Veiled Threat*, Sally Armstrong estimates that eighty percent of women in Pakistan have been victims of domestic cruelty. Sadly, in most cases, police look the other way. In one case when a woman actually burned to death, the police reported it as a cooking accident. Such incidents are often ignored because of the unsubstantiated conclusion connecting the victim's death to her own supposed infidelity. In the rare cases when a woman manages to escape, she is sent back to her husband if caught.

Let us acknowledge the courage of women who have taken matters in their own hands and continue to campaign against honor killing in places such as Palestine, Lebanon, and Jordan.

Backed by organizations such as UNICEF, these brave women are bringing light to the crime of honor killing, and its root cause. It is the concept of male ownership of women and the perception of them as nothing more than property or slaves, which allows this kind of horrible act to occur repeatedly.

I would like to speak to young women living in progressive (Western) countries that have become supporters of Hijab by claiming the Islamic books' references to women's equality with men, and further claiming those books' references to women as the preferred sex in *Allah's* eyes. But how preferred are women really are in the eyes of *Allah*? When based on the Koran's description of creation, God created men from one soul, and women from the same soul, for companionship. I am curious then, is it really women's sole purpose of existence to join with men as second-class citizens?

Women and Circumcision:

Female Genital Mutilation (FGM)

What I am about to discuss may at first seem irrelevant to the subject of Hijab, but I strongly believe in the connection between this gruesome and inhumane act to female submissiveness in Islamic nations around the world.

For centuries, women in Islamic countries have been forced to practice certain rituals, which are designed to please men while keeping women cloistered in darkness, despair, and illiteracy.

Al-Nahdah, a well-known Islamic publication in Malaysia, once wrote about the tradition of circumcision among women in early Islam as they made their *Hijrah*[1]. In this story, a woman by the name of Umma Athiah carried out the job of circumcising girls before their pilgrimage. She was making the cuts too deep, and the Prophet Mohammad asked her to avoid making deep cuts since a shallower

---

[1] *Hijrah* (هِجْرَة) is the migration of the Prophet Muhammad and his followers from Mecca to the city of Medina in AD 622.

cut makes the girls more desirable and provides more pleasure to their husbands.

Centuries apart but consistent with this, doctors have reported their experiences while examining women and young girls from different Arabic and African nations, and reported that women from Sudan have the most horrendous form of circumcision. The procedure performed on Sudanese women is, apparently, many times crueler than what is performed on other women in North Africa. Sudanese take away the entire external portion of the female's genital area; *"cutting off the clitoris, the two major lips (labia majora) and the two minor inner lips (labia minora), and repair the wound. The outer opening of the vagina is the only portion left intact." (Parshall, 2002)*

It is common to stitch the opening too narrow, creating an obstruction on the wedding night. Adding to the brutality, the narrow entry is opened by the husband with a sharp razor or knife. If the poor woman divorces, the insanity continues by re-stitching her opening, and if she re-marries, her already stitched opening is cut apart again.

During a Cairo conference held to discuss the issue of FGM, African women discussed the amount of pain associated with intercourse. In some cases, it takes days or weeks of penetration until a proper opening is created. If the husband is not patient, a sharp knife speeds up the process. They referred to so-called honeymoon centers away from the residential areas, where poor brides could freely scream during intercourse, without the risk of being heard by neighbors.

Religious and cultural reasons support the practice of circumcision. Christa Muller of INTACT, International Initiative Against Female Genital Mutilation (FGM), explains the cultural belief that: "*women who haven't undergone circumcision aren't able to bear children later in life, or uncircumcised women aren't as attractive as those who've been circumcised*". *(Deutsche Welle broadcaster, 2004)*

She further discusses the male role in a woman's sexual destiny. A man wants to affirm the virginity of his bride and be the only one among the two experiencing pleasure. This act of domination comforts him, knowing that his wife will not play the field and the children born to her are his own.

In *The Caged Virgin*, Hirsi Ali refers to girls' circumcision as a way to preserve and ensure their virginity. *"Female circumcision serves two purposes: the clitoris is removed in order to reduce the women's sexuality, and the labia are sewn up in order to guarantee her virginity. "*

In an attempt to bring attention to the cruelty of FGM, she draws a comparison between male and female circumcision:

… if male circumcision meant removing the glans and testicles, and adhering the remains of the penis to the empty sac, the comparison would be valid. Genital mutilation of girls is the most underestimated violation of human rights and women's rights worldwide. (Hirsi Ali, 2004)

In 2002, Amnesty International reported that every year, *"1-1.4 million girls are circumcised and robbed of their genitals."* These women experience a lifetime of suffering during their menses, intercourse, and childbirth, and many of these women lose their firstborn child to suffocation due to a lack of oxygen caused by an artificially narrowed birth canal.

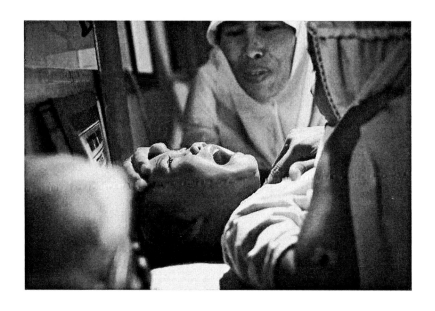

A young girl screams as her genitals are cut during a circumcision.
(Nytimes.com/slideshow/2008/01/20/magazine/

20080120_CIRCUMCISION_SLIDESHOW_6.html)

In March 2005, the Arab News published Maha Akeel's[1] article on female circumcision, indicating that in most cases the girls are not given anesthetics. The older women in the family or neighborhood hold the girl down while another woman carries out the procedure.

---

[1] Maha Akeel, managing editor of The Journal, the print magazine of the Organization of the Islamic Conference.

She uses instruments such as razors, scissors, knives, tin lids or other sharp and often unsterilized objects. One Dutch doctor working in Ghana examined a twenty six-year old woman who was circumcised at age ten; the instrument that had been used was a piece of broken glass. An Indonesian study found that a third of circumcised girls are between five and nine years of age and the rest are mutilated at infancy.

It is not uncommon for girls to die of infection, shock or blood loss. After the procedure, the girl is stitched up and her legs are restrained for forty days.

According to the English-language version of the international UNESCO, FGM is widespread among African, and some Arab and Asian countries. An estimated worldwide 100 to 157 million women and girls are affected by the procedure with two million girls added each year. They contrasted female to male circumcision by emphasizing the potential health hazards and severe damage to female sexual organs, occasionally causing death.

Despite there being a lack of direct reference in either the Koran or the Bible, supporters of FGM claim that:

- Circumcision and infibulations protect women against various illnesses, worms, and discharge.

- Since the clitoris is considered the "male" part of a woman, circumcision converts girls into absolute women and improves their fertility.

- Mutilation protects women against sex outside of marriage by reducing their sexual yearning.

- Infibulated women offer superior sexual pleasure to men.

- Circumcision maintains an ancient tradition and this proves its superiority over modern Western influences.

The roots of these beliefs can be traced back to more structured, dogmatic societies in which severe laws and regulations control women's behavior and movement in order to protect their virginity for the pleasure of men.

What is not considered is the fact that FGM causes serious health problems for women. Among them listed are:

- *Shock due to the severe blood loss;*

- *Blood poisoning, tetanus;*

- *Infection with polio, hepatitis, and HIV;*

- *Problems emptying the bladder; damage to and infection of urinary ducts and the kidneys;*

- *Inflammation of the oviduct and womb;*

- *Heavy bleeding during the monthly period;*

- *Painful sex, especially on the wedding night and after childbirth.*

- *Higher incidences of infant fatality in childbirth due to a vaginal opening that is too small. The tissue has to be cut open to allow the baby to pass through. The scar tissue caused by infibulations is inelastic and causes great pain during birth. Caesarean sections or the use of forceps frequently results. After the birth, the woman is sewn up again, leaving just a pinhead-sized opening.*

(Source: www.dadalos.org)

Common forms of circumcision include: *"rubbing and scraping, stretching, pricking and piercing, incision, and excision"* with cutting gadgets such as a *"penknife, scissor, bamboo knife, razor blade, and needle."*

Unfortunately, there are no proper methods for monitoring FGM and governments have not protected innocent girls by establishing judicial laws to stop such activities. The problem lies in the secrecy and taboo around the entire tribulation, leading to a deficiency in reporting. The United Nations, UNICEF, and the World Health Organization (WHO) consider FGM to be a violation of human rights and propose it be eliminated.

Let us salute the women of the village of Malicounda in Senegal who, in 1997, rebelled against FGM. After realizing that all women around the globe are not subjugated to circumcision they led a heroic effort against FGM, which led to more uprising in neighboring villages and succeeded in banning the practice in almost eighteen villages a year later.

But despite the courageous women taking charge of their bodies and lives, disturbing stories abound, breaking our hearts and leaving dark marks on our souls. It makes us ashamed to be in the same human race as those ignorant and shattered people who carry out the brutal act.

Dr. Winnie Tay, director of Plan International in Sierra Leone, describes a video of an Ethiopian circumcision[1].

...the child in the video is eight years old. Today is her birthday. Her mother takes her by the hand and leads her to a hut at the edge of the village. Inside the hut she is tied to a chair with her legs splayed. An old woman clutching a rusty razor tells her to be brave and not to make a noise. Then she grasps the skin above the child's clitoris and begins cutting. The child screams in agony while the woman slices off piece after piece: The hood of the clitoris, the clitoris itself, the labia minora, the labia majora. She closes the gaping bloody wound with three thorns and slathers it with what looks like herbs and raw eggs. The child is removed to a mat, her legs are tied together, and she is told that now, she is a woman. (Armstrong, 2002)

Millions of other female children have undergone similar procedures, and live to inherit a painful life every time they urinate, menstruate, have intercourse or give birth. They may die from shock, infection or excess bleeding. My prayers are always with them, wherever they may be.

---

[1] As it is described in *Veiled Threat* by Sally Armstrong

CHAPTER III

POWER & LAW

"But words are things, and a small drop of ink, falling

like dew upon a thought, produces that which makes

thousands, perhaps millions, think."

Lord Byron

Like any other Good Old Boys club, Islamic men have decided to keep the power and honor to themselves. They have held the fate of women in their hands and stripped them of their communal rights, remaining satisfied as long as their prejudiced and unbalanced power is not challenged.

In order to gain absolute power, one must create fear. There is nothing more powerful than the fear of the unknown, the wrath of *Allah*. A benevolent, merciful God on all accounts, except when women are the subject, and on matters connected to honor and sexuality.

Women's Legal Testimony

In most Islamic countries, a woman's testimony is limited to civil cases and cases that are personal in nature. In Saudi Arabia women are unable to testify in criminal cases. There are four reasons given for this, elucidated by Jean Sasson, in her book, *Princess:*

- *Women are much more emotional than men and will, as a result of their emotions, distort their testimony.*
- *Women do not participate in public life, so they will not be capable of understanding what they observe.*
- *Women are dominated completely by men, who by the grace of God are deemed superior, therefore, women will give testimony according to what the last man told them.*
- *Women are forgetful and their testimony cannot be considered reliable. (Sasson, 1992)*

From an early age, men are taught to exercise their superiority over women, particularly their mothers, sisters, and wives. For centuries, men have been trained to regard women as subservient with diminutive worth, existing only for service and to bring comfort to men's surroundings.

Rape and Islamic Law

Women and girls in Islamic societies may face incrimination if they report an act of rape or sexual attack. For a woman to prove she has been raped requires the testimony of four male witnesses, as stated in the Koran. The eyewitnesses must be Muslim and in good standing. If the rape victim cannot provide four credible observers or the confession of the rapist himself, she is assumed guilty.

Take Arpita Mukherjee's 2008 article on Saudi Arabia's rape victims:

...Saudi Arabia's Higher Judicial Council has actually sentenced a rape victim to receive 200 lashes and prison while the perpetrators of humanity's most heinous crime were allowed to walk free. The 19-year-old Shiite woman who was raped by six armed men was originally sentenced to receive 90 lashes for traveling in the car of an 'unrelated male' at the time of the rape. However, after the woman had the temerity of not unquestioningly submitting herself to be tortured as punishment of being raped, the judges on Saudi Arabia's Higher Judicial Council more than doubled her punishment

*for attempting to influence the judiciary through the media.
(http://www.themuslimwoman.org/entry/rape-victim-ordered-200-lashes-and-prison-by-saudi-judges/)*

**Rape victim ordered 200 lashes and imprisonment by Saudi judges.
(Themuslimwoman.org)**

Sex Trafficking in the Islamic World

The ruling *mullahs* in Iran see to it that women are humiliated and punished by all types of cruelties. It is not surprising to see a great number of young girls from rural areas and poor urban neighborhoods run away from home in hopes of finding happiness elsewhere, which makes them more vulnerable to falling into the hands of sex slave operations and organized prostitution rings, called *kharabat [brothel]*.

The most common victims are young women from underprivileged and rural areas, some girls being as young as eight years of age. One method of recruitment is to find those who have run away from their already intolerable and abusive homes in search of freedom.

Donna M. Hughes claims that in today's Iran, as cited in *Women in Islam,* these organized brothels sell young women and girls to prostitution, further demoralizing their existence as women. Unfortunately, some Iranian government officials are among the criminals, not only enjoying the financial gains of this lucrative – and immoral – business, but also participating in the abuse and sexual acts.

In Iran for twenty-five years, the ruling mullahs have enforced humiliating and sadistic rules and punishments on women and girls, enslaving them in a gender apartheid system of segregation, forced veiling, second-class status, lashing, and stoning to death. Joining a global trend, the fundamentalists have added another way to dehumanize women and girls: buying and selling them for prostitution. (Speaker-Yuan, 2005)

It is impossible to find the exact numbers for such activities but there have been numerous indications of sex slave trafficking among organizations located in Iran, Pakistan, and Arab islands in the Persian Gulf. Child prostitution rings are not, however, a problem existing only in Islamic countries; this is a worldwide problem, with sex slavery occurring in *"Albania, former Yugoslavia, Azerbaijan, Afghanistan, Tajikistan, Chechnya, Sierra Leone, Sudan, Congo, various countries in Latin America, China, Vietnam, Philippines, et cetera." (Speaker-Yuan, 2005)*

The cruelty continues when arrested prostitutes are forced to have sex with their captors, which in some cases include *mullahs* as well as the arresting officers. Let us remember that these women have virtually no legal recourse, because of the Islamic law requiring four male witnesses to bring about a rape charge.

In a town near the capital city of Iran, a group of senior government officials were arrested on charges of selling runaway girls to organized prostitution operations. These girls had sought shelter in government funded "morality" houses. The ruling government of Iran, possibly in an attempt to prevent the spread of HIV and other venereal diseases, had created these special houses to shelter prostitutes and runaways. However, the outcome was to further suppress women and control their destiny by selling some of them off. (Speaker-Yuan, 2005)

The Islamic fundamentalism widespread in Iran has gone far beyond religious conservatism and, as mentioned in *Women in Islam*, it has formed a *"political movement with a political ideology that considers women inherently inferior in intellectual and moral capacity." (Speaker-Yuan, 2005)*

Stoning

One of the punishments for both male and female adulterers is death by stoning. This gruesome method can be traced back to the Dark Ages but is still practiced in fundamentalist Islamic countries today. Ordinary people in the community take part by bandaging, tying, and mummifying the victims in white sheets and placing them in holes dug according to each person's measurement, and then burying them in the hole from the waist down. Hundreds of people then throw stones at the victims. In the book *Rage Against the Veil*, the author explains that there are *"rules for the stones, too. It can't just be any rock. The stone has to be big enough to really hurt the person, but not so big that it would kill them in one throw."* (Darabi, 1999)

Images from a stoning. (Dhushara.com/paradoxhtm/vale/stoning.jpg)

Throughout the ordeal, the stone-throwers take breaks to adjust the wilted bodies by standing them upright in their holes in order to ensure that the bodies are receiving the incoming stones. Once the white sheets are tattered and red with blood:

...the sheets and bandages start to tear and blood spills out on to the ground. When the people figure out that the woman has died, they bury her and walk away... There is no doctor present to make sure that the person is dead. Sometimes the victims are still alive when they are covered with dirt. As people leave the stoning, they laugh and talk and tell stories like those that are returning from a trip to the carnival. (Darabi, 1999)

As recently as 2009, news of an Iranian stoning appeared in *Kayhan*[1], the Iranian State run newspaper. The article refers to a twenty-year-old woman who lived through a stoning and woke up at a morgue as

[1] Kayhan – (Persian: کیهان, English: *universe*) an influential newspaper in Iran. Directly under the supervision of the Office of the Supreme Leader, it is regarded to be "the most conservative Iranian newspaper."

they were preparing her for burial. The woman, accused of adultery and sentenced to stoning until death, was recovering at the local hospital located in Bukan, Kordestan, awaiting her fate as the local district attorney requested a pardon from the Islamic judicial system.

Women in Islamic Law

There are several laws specifically issued that further limit Iranian women living under Shari'a Law. Lawyers and human rights activists focusing on Iranian women's civil rights, among them, Mehrangiz Kar in her Farsi book *Research About Violence Against Women in Iran,* points to several articles of the Islamic Republic Law codes describing punishment for crimes and misbehavior related to women.

Consider the following articles of Civil and Penal Law that I discovered during my research for this book.

Article 1210:1 of Civil Law focuses on the interpretation of the current legal age for boys and girls. According to the Islamic decree, which dictates Iran's judicial system, girls are considered adults at age nine while boys are not considered adults until age fifteen, and this in turn means that children of this age must stand to defend themselves in civil as well as criminal courts of law.

Under the Islamic Republic's rule over the last thirty years, the people of Iran have been witness to numerous horrific crimes related to juvenile girls' so-called adultery and breach of chastity. Thanks to reporters and journalists such as Asieh Amini[1] we learn of some horrific life stories, which would have remained untold otherwise. According to the report, Atefah Sahaaleh was not different from any other 16-year-old teenager, full of dreams and aspirations. She lost her mother in early childhood and due to circumstances beyond her control, she lacked constant supervision in her daily life.

At thirteen, Atefah received her first one hundred lashes from the same *'moral police guard'* who raped her. She continued being raped and exploited by a 51-year-old married man, who himself had children and who happened to be a former Revolutionary Guard. Sad to say, her rapist's only punishment was ninety or so lashes, administered by his former friends from the Revolutionary Guard.

---

[1] Asieh Amini: an accomplished journalist, published poet, and courageous activist.

Atefah's general situation is not too different from that of millions of other teenagers across the globe and is certainly nothing to be hung for. Nevertheless, she was sentenced to hang by the neck in the town square of Neka, Iran, August 2004. Although the Iranian Islamic judicial system has promised to abide by the *International Convention on Civil and Political Rights* and not execute youngsters under the age of eighteen, Atefah was hung at age sixteen.

While investigating the case, Amini came across birth and death certificates kept by Atefah's father, which validated her age at her death as sixteen. The local bloodthirsty judge, teamed up with his Revolutionary Guards, not only disregarded the victim's birth record, but ignored the capital punishment grace period by ordering an abrupt hanging without notifying her relatives for a last farewell.

The local police were also to blame for Atefah's repeated rapes, assaults, and lashings for ridiculous charges over the years. After Atefah's death, the judge's answer to such questionable and abrupt sentencing was that they *[legal authorities]* thought that she was a 22-year-old married adulterer. The cause written on her official death sentence was *"crimes against chastity."*

Articles 63 - 113 of Islamic Penal Code describe sentencing of up to one hundred lashes for those who participate in sexual activities outside of wedlock. Islamic Penal Codes refer to the act of rape as punishable by death. However, it is very difficult, often impossible for a woman to prove she has been raped. If a woman is unable to provide proof of her rape, she faces punishment for accusing a man of rape, as well as the punishment for being involved in an illicit sexual act, which in some cases mean receiving lashes or being stoned to death.

Articles 1102, 1104, 1114, 1115, & 1116 of Family Law grant the husband authority to choose his wife's place of residence, and further mandate women to obey and seek permission from their husbands on all matters related to their place of residence.

Article 18:3 of Authorization Law indicates that married women must acquire their husbands' written permission to obtain passport prior to exiting the country. A supplement to the article prohibits single women from exiting without permission, which means these women must seek the permission of their fathers or brothers.

Article 1117 of Family Law gives husbands the right to

forbid their wives the pursuit of professions that the husbands have deemed unsuitable for the family honor.

Article 638 of Islamic Penal Code describes the punishment for women who appear unveiled in public. They are subject to a 10 to

60 day jail sentence or cash equivalent. Women must follow mandatory rules concerning their wardrobes, veils, and the assigned colors. A women's magazine, referring to the subject of Hijab and its allocated colors, indicated that women in Iran had been stripped of the simple ability to choose the color of their wardrobe since everyone else had made that decision for them. Black is the Islamic Government's recommended color.

Article 99 of Islamic Penal Code describes the harsh punishment of stoning for a married woman found guilty of sexual activities outside of marriage. It is also significant to mention that the Iranian judicial system grants husbands permission to punish their wives as described in the next article.

Article 630 of Islamic Penal Code permits a husband to kill his adultering wife and the other man, as necessary.

Article 441 of Islamic Penal Code penalizes men with a small fine for jeopardizing a girl's virginity by finger. This law appears to

protect young women but the insult and degradation lies in the idea that a girl with "damaged" virginity will not be able to find a good husband as a result.

Article 487 of Islamic Penal Code describes various fines for women who abort their fetuses at different developmental stages. According to the Islamic law, women are not free to have abortions; it is considered murder and they are judged as criminals.

Article 220 of Islamic Penal Code is in direct contrast to the previously mentioned article. In this law, the Islamic Republic of Iran allows fathers and paternal grandfathers to kill their children and grandchildren by their own hands, if they deem it necessary.

Article 1133 of Civil Law exempts men from presenting evidence in divorce cases. Men, by law, are allowed to divorce their wives at anytime.

In the Koran and under Islamic law, husbands have permission to terminate their marriage and abandon their wives at their discretion, by simply pronouncing, *"she is divorced."* the Koran has taken exceptional measures to ensure the absolute power of men over women by repeating men's rights to divorce in over a dozen verses.

Article 1169 of Islamic Family Law only allows a mother to have custody of her male children for up to two years of age and of female children up to seven years of age. Afterwards, it is the father, by law, who receives full custody. If the mother remarries or is deemed insane during her custody period, the father or his family takes full custody of the children.

Women Speaking Up

Jennifer Hurley, in *Islam – Opposing Viewpoints*, proclaims that only Muslim women can break the vicious cycle of inaction and stagnation:

Interestingly, the one place where this is very practicable is the United States, because here putting belief into action is not a distant mirage. Again, only we Muslim women, through education, action, and courage can reclaim what in actuality are our God given rights. (Hurley, 2001)

If we assume for a second that all men desire to act out their fantasy to dominate others, especially women, then we can believe that

Islam has taken one giant step towards granting those wishes to Muslim men. The burden of proof and further education remains the responsibility of courageous men and women, to expose the terrifying consequences resulting from the sick and twisted ideas of such dominance.

Islamic women who wear Hijab and possess a reasonable degree of freedom in choosing their appearance in public may have romanticized Islam's and the Prophet's approach to Hijab as a celestial and divine act. They forget about men's earthly conduct, including their violent behavior against Muslim women.

In my opinion, Islam is a militant, masculine, and chauvinistic religion, with Koranic verses condoning that behavior.

Kill them [infidels], wherever you may come upon them, and seize them, and confine them, and lie in wait for them at every conceivable place. (Koran, 9:5)

When you meet those who disbelieve in war, smite them at their neck. (Koran, 47:4)

Economic factors are the core indicator of women's lack of autonomy. Koranic law only allows women one-half of the inheritance given to their male family members, and this puts them at an immediate financial disadvantage. By granting men unlimited power over women, Islam tips the balance between the two and pushes a wedge between the sexes. Because women do not have financial autonomy, men are given license to exercise unfair practices.

Men are the protectors and maintainers of women, because Allah has given the one of them [men] to excel the other [women], and because they support them from their means. Therefore, the righteous women are devoutly obedient, and guard in (the husband's) absence what Allah would have them guard... (Koran, 4:34)

According to a *Hadith* (3.48.826)[1], the Prophet asked, *"Is it true that the witness of a woman is equal to half of a man?"* As women nodded, he claimed: *"It is because of the shortfall of a woman's mind."* The Prophet

---

[1] As cited in Voices Behind the Veil: The World of Islam Through the Eyes of Women, (2003). By Ergun Mehmet Caner – General Editor.

120 | Under the Veil

also explained that due to defects in the female mind and intellect, they do not equate to men.

Doubtless, in the Koran's thousand or so pages we can find lines referring to women's equality; after all, the Prophet was married to the wealthiest and most influential woman in the region. What good would it do him if he was not respectful to women during those years, especially when he was the sole beneficiary of the inheritance? However, the sections related to women's obedience and their punishments for disobedience far surpass those granting equal rights.

In support of Islam, Lisa Spray, in her book, *Heart's Surprise*, indicates that during the Koran's development and exposure, slavery was a common behavior among people. The Koran inaugurated a social order where slavery was phased out. She praises *Allah* for Islam's worldwide accomplishment in this matter. How naïve and one sided we must be, believing such propaganda when millions of Muslim women across the world have been subjugated to honor killing, forced marriages, circumcisions, and in-house imprisonment. How could we not identify these acts as slavery, or worse?

I feel ashamed to associate with such self-righteous women, at the expense of the millions of victimized women around the world. We must speak on their behalf and defend their vulnerable positions by exposing the extremely dangerous environment in which they live. Their lives are hanging by a thread, everyday.

Based on the core value system taught in Islam, there will be war and suffering as long as there are non-Muslims in the world. It is Islamic imperative that everyone converts to the faith. The Koran considers people who leave Islam to be traitors, and treason is punishable by death: *"...but if they turn renegades, seize them and slay them wherever ye find them."* (Koran, 4.89) Alarmingly, Islamic violence is increasing. As cited in *Introducing Issues With Opposing Viewpoints: Islam*, Mahmud Hassan, a member of the Muslim Canadian Congress, states:

We are all – Muslim and non-Muslim alike – facing a tremendous crisis. One and a half billion people are roaring down a highway at 150 miles an hour with no driver. Unless something happens soon, a crash is inevitable. (Friedman, 2006)

In Iran, Afghanistan, Pakistan, and the Arabic and African countries, Islam has created one giant prison for women, confined to the four corners of their homes and stripped of their basic rights. These women do not even have the common rights granted to the rest of us in the free world including: the freedom to choose how to live, where to work, when to travel or even to go out shopping or make basic decisions about finances, children, and the like. Lauri Friedman further describes that Islamic laws are the opposite of Western laws, which protect the rights of individuals. Islamic countries create laws protecting the rights of the family. The rights of women are defined by their roles as daughters, wives, and mothers, yet they are denied equal status in cases of divorce and child custody.

My Own Experience

For a short period in the early 1980s, I found myself at risk of being trapped in Iran, unable to exit the country without written permission from my husband at the time. Departing with my daughter made matters even more complicated since he suspected that I would not be coming back. Iranian law grants husbands full authority to permit or deny their wives to travel abroad. Decades later, the bitter memory remains.

I can still recall the exact words exchanged and the pathetic scene created at the airport, where I remained silent and still in the face of his accusations that my daughter and I would not return to Iran. He openly threatened to revoke his permission, preventing me from departing, and worse, keeping my daughter with him and prohibiting her from traveling with me. All this he could have easily done since Iranian law gives fathers ultimate custody over children.

I still remember how helpless and defeated I felt during those hours in the airport, waiting to leave the country. I promised myself never again to become such an easy target for aggression. I also promised myself never to take my freedom in the United States for granted.

CHAPTER IV

CONTINUED HUMILIATION

"How happy is a bird who has never seen a cage?

Even happier is the one who has fled the cage.

They have broken our wings and opened the doors of the cages."

Sadegh Sarmad[1]

Once Allah's Apostle [Prophet Mohammad] went out to the Musalla (to offer the prayer) o 'Id-al-Adha or Al-Fitr prayer. Then he passed by the women and said, "O women! Give alms, as I have seen that the majority of the dwellers of Hell-fire were you (women)." They asked, "Why is it so, O Allah's Apostle?" He replied, "You curse frequently and are ungrateful to your husbands. I have not seen anyone more deficient in intelligence and religion than you. A cautious sensible man could be led astray by some of you." The women asked, "O Allah's Apostle! What is deficient in our intelligence and religion?" He said, "Is not the evidence of two women equal

---

[1] Sadegh Sarmad, a Contemporary Iranian Poet.

to the witness of one man?" They replied in the affirmative. He said, "This is the deficiency in her intelligence. Isn't it true that a woman can neither pray nor fast during her menses?" The women replied in the affirmative. He said, "This is the deficiency in her religion."

(Sahih Bukhari, translated by Khan, vol. 1, book 6, no. 301)

Islamic men, including the Prophet Mohammad, have shamefully bashed women for centuries. The Prophet's *Allah* protected him repeatedly by delivering holy verses as quickly as Mohammad needed to conquer women. After the Prophet's first wife died, it was well known that his harem was occupied by more than a dozen wives, excluding the young concubines. *Allah* gave his Prophet special privileges to marry more than four wives, as was the limit for other Muslims. Of course, certain criteria had to be met but there was nothing asked that the Prophet couldn't meet.

Allah made him exempt from paying a bride price, mandatory for other Muslim men. In his 50's, Prophet Mohammad married the six year old Aisha. He gave himself permission to sleep with his soldiers' and adopted son's wives. The Prophet also cherry picked some desirable women while conquering other nations. He claimed the captured women as his wives, unless they refused to embrace Islam, in which case they became his concubines.

As the story is told, when Mohammad conquered *Khaybar*, a Jewish settlement, he ordered the torture and decapitation of the tribe's chief. The Prophet's men told him that the chief had just married a beautiful brown-eyed woman. Mohammad sent one of his disciples to fetch the young bride. It is said that the Prophet consummated with the seventeen-year-old widow, named Safiyya, that very same night, without observing the grace period instructed by the Koran before sleeping with widows.

POWERFUL WORDS FROM THE SKY ABOVE

Male domination existed in the pre-Islamic era, and sadly, the Prophet Mohammad did not do much to discourage men from being sex-crazed. The Prophet himself had a healthy appetite when it came to women. Whenever he lusted over someone new, he justified it with an incoming verse inspired by an angel of *Allah*. Sometimes the verse was for him alone, and sometimes he opened the door, blessing other men to share the good fortune.

Exclusive to him was the case of Zainab, the wife of his adopted son Zeyd. Mohammad was struck with a passionate desire for Zainab when he visited his adopted son's home and found her alone without her husband. Apparently, Mohammad demonstrated his desire for her, since his adopted son, heartbroken, and, out of respect for his father, offered to give up his wife to the Prophet by divorcing her. Conveniently, for Mohammad *Allah* came to the rescue by delivering a verse encouraging him to take Zainab's hand in marriage. This verse appears in the Koran 33:37 & 38:

> *... So when Zeyd had performed the necessary formality (of divorce) from her, we gave her unto thee in marriage, so that (henceforth) there may be no sin for believers in respect of wives of their adopted sons, when the latter have performed the necessary formality (of release) from them. The commandment of Allah must be fulfilled. There is no reproach for the Prophet in that which Allah maketh his due. (Parshall, 2002)*

As explained in *Women and the Koran:*

> *Mohammad went on to marry others and his Allah continued to cover his tracks with new verses. In fact it appears that the supreme deity would take a personal interest in the sex life of his Prophet. (Hekmat, 1997)*

The Prophet and the *mullahs* needed to legitimize their chauvinistic and excessively sexual behavior toward women, or they would have disappeared into history as the corrupt and perverted men that they are.

Was Heaven Made Only for Islamic Men?

In addition to men's earthly supply of wives and concubines, the Prophet and the Koran promised a gift of some seventy-two flawless, dark-eyed virgins awaiting them in heaven. *"...there shall be virgins chaste and fair... Dark eyed virgins sheltered in their tents whom neither man nor Jin [Genie] will have touched before." (Koran 55:70-77)* These women, called *houris*, do not get pregnant, menstruate, perspire, or become ill. Numerous verses in the Koran, such as Sura's 37, 38, 44, 52, 55, and 56, speak of beautiful virgins awaiting men in heaven.

> *...We created the houris [the beautiful women] and made them virgins, loving companions for those on the right hand."* (56:7-40). *...They shall recline on couches ranged in rows. To dark-eyed houris we shall wed them...* (52:17-20)

> *(source: http://www.flex.com/~jai/satyamevajayate/heaven.html)*

In answer to the question, *"How many wives will the believers be allowed to have in Paradise?"* Islamic scholar Shaykh Gibril Haddad[1] referred to a *Hadith* told by Bukhari[2]:

Each man among them shall have two wives, the marrow of each of the two wives' shanks will be seen glimmering under the flesh, and there is not in all Paradise a single unmarried man. They will have up to a hundred concubines in Paradise while the Shuhada' [martyrs] shall have seventy-two wives, numbers indicating abundance rather than an exact quantity, and Allah knows best. (Source: http://www.livingislam.org)

In *Veiled Threat*, Sally Armstrong refers to Dr. Elmasry's[3] claim that, *"the interpretation that refers to seventy-two virgins comes from an obscure book written by an ancient scholar using his own opinion of the wording in the Koran." (Armstrong, 2002)*

---

[1] Dr. Gibril Fouad Haddad (born 1960) is an Arabic translator.

[2] Muhammad ibn Ismail al-Bukhari, popularly known as Al-Bukhari or Imam Bukhari (810-870), was a famous Sunni Islamic scholar of Bukharian ancestry.

[3] Dr. Elmasry, National President, Canadian Islamic Congress.

It is quoted by the Islamic scholar, Ibn Kathir[1], in his *Tafsir [Koranic Commentary]* of Koran's Sura 55:72:

It was mentioned by Daraj Ibn Abi Hatim, that Abu al-Haytham 'Adullah Ibn Wahb narrated from Abu Sa'id al-Khudhri, who heard the Prophet Mohammad saying, 'The smallest reward for the people of Heaven is an abode where there are eighty thousand servants and seventy-two houri,...' (Source: http://www.qtafsir.com)

The Koran's heavenly enjoyments are for men, while their wives, in Heaven, are expected to remain calm and obedient as they witness their husbands seeking pleasure in the company of the *houris.*

The Prophet further established his dominance over his wives and forbade them to remarry after his death. He had, of course, received a Koranic endorsement: *"The Prophet is closer to the believers than they are and his wives are their mothers." (Koran, 33:6)* With that said,

---

[1] Ibn Kathir (b. 1301 in Busra, Syria) was renowned for his great memory regarding the sayings of Prophet Muhammad and the entire *Qur'an.*

no Muslim in his right mind would dare approach the deceased Prophet's wife, even the very young Aisha.

Despite suicide being expressly forbidden in the Koran, there is evidence of a somewhat new and disturbing trend of female suicide bombers. If male martyrs can receive seventy-two *houris* in the afterlife, what are these female martyrs offered? What do the shameless fanatics do to recruit desperate young women to take part in suicide bombing and destroy the lives of innocent people?

Women as Property

Islamic fundamentalists consider woman to be a man's property and, throughout her life, ownership shifts from father to husband. This idea of ownership has been traced back to early stages of human evolution. In *Women and the Koran*, a reference to an illustration by Charles Darwin indicates:

> *The same attitude is seen in many animal species. For example, a male ape that has several females in his possession will not permit any other male to approach them, even if the males are the offspring of his own females. (Hekmat, 1997)*

Hekmat further indicates: *"...the inflexible laws of Islam have deprived half of the population of their equal rights"*. According to the Koran: *"The male is in charge of the female." (Koran, 4:34)*

Worse even than property, women have been considered toys:

Abu Bakr Ahmed Ibn Abd Allah (one of the Muslim scholars) said; "Umar (the Just Khalif) was once talking when his wife interjected, so he said to her, "You are a toy, if you are needed we will call you" Amru Bin Al Aas (also a Khalif) said, "Women are toys, so choose." (Kanz-el-Ummal, Vol. 21, Hadith No. 919). Mohammed himself said, "The woman is a toy, whoever takes her let him care for her," according to Ahmed Zaki Tuffaha on page 180 of the book Al-Mar'Allah wal-islam (The Woman and Islam). (http://www.arabicbible.com/christian/Women_in_Islam.htm)

In Search of Identity

Ultimately, it doesn't matter how women appear in public - showing their bodies or not - as long as they are able to choose for themselves. It is essential to not to have mandatory requirements, which limit physical and mental abilities as well as allow men to perceive women as useless, submissive and easy prey.

In the 2008 issue of *Insight Publication*, Manal Omar describes that educated women who enjoy freedom to choose wear Hijab for a variety of reasons. Therefore, it is wrong to conclude that all Hijab-wearing women are all oppressed. I support this viewpoint as long as the conscious decision made by this minority of women exercising their freedom of choice does not hurt the majority of women without the freedom to choose. It is sinful for free spirited women to be used as instruments of propaganda for tyrants of Islamic fundamentalism.

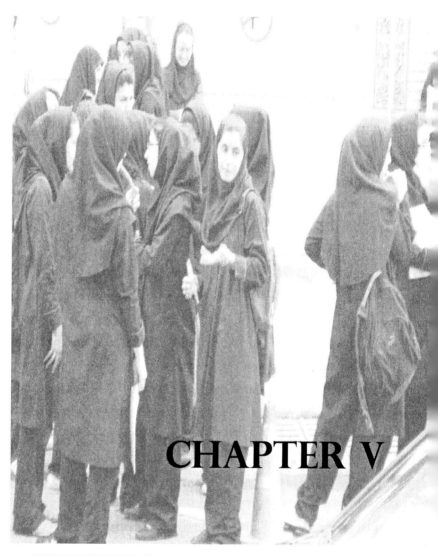

CHAPTER V

WOMEN IN BONDAGE:

A GLOBAL ISSUE

Even in the 21st century, Gendercide exists. Economically and educationally deprived women in Islamic societies continue to suffer in silence because of institutional censorship and cultural conditioning but conscientious journalists continue to report on the despicable crimes committed against women every day. It is my wish for the reader to become aware of current issues for women in various Islamic countries around the world.

IRAN

With its 98% Shiite population, Iran is ruled by an Islamic constitution under Shari'a law, but because Iranian culture puts such a high value on education, the number of educated young women is on the rise. Over 60% of university-level entrants are women, as well as 70% of recent graduates. This worries the controversial President Mahmud Ahmadinejad, who, along with the ruling Ayatollahs and the hardliner government, anticipates a major clash as these educated women will want to participate in all aspects of personal decision-making, as well as reshaping of the country.

Since the 1979 Islamic Revolution, women in Iran have been allowed to work outside the home, but Ahmadinejad, through his speeches and the words of his advisors, has encouraged women to limit their careers to the areas of health and education, and devote the majority of their time to raising children. He has strongly advised the women who work in technical and engineering fields to perform their employment duties from home in order to minimize their interaction with men.

The Islamic establishment continues to find ridiculous ways of insulting women and reminding them who is in charge. In December of 2009, the head of the state-run television station appeared in a public service announcement banning women from wearing makeup: *"It's illegal and against Shari'a law."* Although this particular case seems laughable, women are still victimized by police brutality, lashing, and imprisonment, not only for holding anti-establishment political and social views but also for not following the Islamic dress code and dressing in what is called "bad hijab".

Hijab itself has become more malleable in certain progressive parts of Iran. In the wealthier, more educated area of northern Tehran, women can be seen showing some hair under loose, brightly colored scarves. Because of massive campaigns after the Revolution promoting fertility and population growth, most of Iran's people are less than 30 years of age. This young, hip and cyber-connected population has been pushing the rules, and some superficial freedoms have been gained. However, a run-in with the wrong legal authorities may still results in abduction, imprisonment, and rape, all in the name of Islamic authority.

The Iranian government's recent propaganda against "bad hijab" appears in daily newspapers. An article in June of 2010, openly invites women to wear proper Hijab for their salvation. According to the government, wearing make-up is an "un-Islamic" behavior and causes women to become depressed by premature aging. To continue with the humiliation of women accusing them of having "bad hijab" the law enforcement in charge of the ordeal, has set up cameras throughout the city watching men in cars who inappropriately approach or seek company of women with whom they have no relation. At first glance, it appears that this law enforcement activity targets and penalizes men for their actions by impounding their cars, but in fact the penalty and shame is focused on women because the sign claims women as "Chattel" defined as "movable property". Therefore, women are the property of a man, most likely her father if young or un-married, or husband if married.

Photo from the front page of the Iranian Newspaper, Omid Javan displays a locked up and marked car by the municipal police displaying a sign that says
"OFFENDERS OF CHATTEL"

In addition, government operated newspapers have started a systematic campaign further eliminating women's already limited freedom. They complain that too many university classrooms are occupied by women. The government blames women for the country's high unemployment rate, claiming women's active participation in the work force has "taken away" men's rights to those jobs. Veteran members of the parliament and the clergy, in their periodic interviews with reporters, urge parents to marry off their daughters while they are still in middle school in order to further secure their safekeeping. Their rationale is simply and satanically genius; the young girl is legally married and protected from any "foul play". Her husband will claim her as soon as her father and husband decide she is ready to leave her father's house, which leaves the girl with no time to explore the world or to seek higher education. Shari'a law mandates that wives must obtain their husbands' approval for outside employment.

A veteran member of the Iranian Parliament, Mousa Ghorbani, in his interview with the Daily Newspaper, *Omid Javan*[1] in June of 2010, recalls his recent trip to Mecca and his fascination with Saudi Arabian laws on treatment of women. He expresses his satisfaction for the absence of women in work places. Ghorbani explains that

---

[1] Omid Javan – Iranian Newspaper, 676 issue.

most of Iran's problems would go away if only they applied Saudi laws concerning women in Iran. Clergies with government backing are encouraging married women to not only accept their husbands' multiple wives, but also actively seek new wives for their husbands. Wishful lawmakers hope for women to voluntarily embrace the Koranic multiple wives law and get "onboard with the plan" of satisfying their husbands' sexual urges, while simultaneously helping the government to reduce the excess number of temporary marriages [Mut'a], widely practiced by the Muslim married men.

The article: "Women to accept men's multiple marriages"

Nevertheless, in 2010's March 8th International Women's Rights Day, activists publicly declared that, *"Iran should stop infringing on women's rights and take immediate steps to meet Iranian women's demands for full equality."*

THE ARAB COUNTRIES

Despite the **Saudi Arabian** government's endorsement of the *UN Covenant for the Elimination of all forms of Discrimination Against Women (CEDAW)* in September of 2001, the situation for Saudi women has barely improved. Under Koranic, Shari'a, and Saudi law, men are allowed four wives and can marry Christians or Jews, while women are only allowed to marry Muslim men.

Generally, Saudi women must quietly tolerate their male family members' violence against them. Most laws are one-sided, protecting men. In divorce cases, a woman receives only three months of maintenance payment before her husband or his family takes over full custody of the child. Clearly, women's financial shortcomings (such as receiving only half of their inheritance and a lack of job opportunities) leave women at a great disadvantage. Not uncommon is the story of a 26-year-old Egyptian women who holds a degree in law but has to clean bathrooms to support herself. In Saudi Arabia, she is not permitted to work as a lawyer. In this case, her only limitation is the discrimination against her because of her sex.

Because Saudi Arabia's extreme form of Hijab (the *niqab*) covers the face, showing only the eyes, Saudi women are at a political disadvantage. They are denied from having national identification cards because of the law against showing women's unveiled faces. Despite the hopes of progressive Saudi's, the government confirmed that women were not allowed to either vote or run in the first nationwide election held in 2005. Interior Minister Prince Nayef, in his interview with a Kuwaiti newspaper, proclaimed, *"I don't think that women's participation is possible."*

In neighboring **Bahrain**, the *Gulf Daily News* reported in March of 2010 on a gang-rape trial that was requested to be dismissed from court, because the defense lawyer called it *"harmless fun."* Shamefully, the defense lawyer was female.

Due to the absence of a decent security in today's **Iraq**, Muslim and Christian women have to wear Hijab despite the Women's League slogan: *"No to the compulsory veil."* In August of 2003, *BBC News*, quoted a woman saying, *"If you walk on the street without a veil now you can get killed."* Professional Iraqi women, especially, are victims of assassinations and abductions, both in and outside of the country. Women's gathering places, such as hair salons, have been targeted for violence. It is disturbing to know that the violence against women in Iraq has been considered a secondary issue and a mere distraction to the core post-war issues.

In 2009, *Huffington Post* reported on a brother stabbing and killing his pregnant sister in order to restore his family's honor. The young woman had apparently moved back to her childhood home after an argument with her husband months earlier. Her brother, however, suspected foul play. *"The 28-year-old married woman was five months pregnant and stabbed repeatedly in the face, neck, abdomen, and back as well as being hacked up with a meat cleaver, according to a government pathologist."*

As recently as April 2010, *CNN News* told the story of a 12-year-old girl from **Yemen** died from internal bleeding a few days after her wedding. Her injuries were related to sexual intercourse with her new husband, almost twice her age. The legal age for marriage in Yemen is in dispute and there have been other recent news reports of young girls being raped and beaten after their weddings.

In May of 2001, **Lebanese** women held a conference to find ways to stop honor killing at the hands of their male relatives. But in **Jordan**, which is perceived to be a more progressive country compared to its neighbors, honor killings are not considered a severely punishable crime.

ASIA

Afghanistan is an overwhelmingly Muslim country, but underneath the central force of Islam, the diversity of multi-tribal and multi-ethnic societies are highly influenced by honor and blood ties. Despite the Mongol invasion of Afghanistan in the early 13th Century and the extending will of the Russian and British Empires in the 19th Century, Islam has played a key role in the formation of Afghan history.

Before the 1996 takeover by Taliban forces, women in Afghanistan were educated and made up a large part of the work force, with half the students and 60% of the teachers at Kabul University being women. However, almost literally overnight, the Taliban stripped Afghani women of basic human rights and banned them from public life. Women were forced to stay at home under the guard of their husbands and fathers, and could only leave the house with male permission, covered up by a *burqa*. Afghani women were thrust into the dark ages by the Taliban's brutal rules.

Photo from a video film by RAWA - http://www.rawa.org/murder-w.htm

Taliban publicly execute woman - AP, November 17, 1999

After the 2001 U.S. overthrow of the Taliban, things began to look up for Afghani women. They could again return to work and school and were no longer obliged to wear the *burqa*. Nevertheless, in the rural areas living under heavy Taliban influence, women continue to suffer; they are still forced to cover up and remain at home, and nearly one thousand girl's schools have been burned down. As recently as 2009, two young girls on their way to school were sprayed with acid.

In August of 2009, President Hamid Karzai passed a law that was again a step backwards for Afghani women. This law allowed men to stop feeding their wives if they refused sex, while at the same time requiring a woman to have her husband's permission to work. Laws like this leave women little choice within an abusive marriage and self-immolation is on the rise. Women who run away from domestic violence are returned when caught, and honor killing continues.

Despite social and cultural stigma, women's shelters have been created and battered women are arriving, desperate for help. These shelters are generally perceived as un-Islamic because tribal leaders typically resolve all familial disputes, and the outcomes nearly always favor the men. Many women fear to speak out about their abuse because of cultural shame and a fear of retaliation.

Politically, in Afghanistan, women are still uncertain about their fate. *Women for Women International*, in its winter 2010 issue, referred to the August 2009 election and reported *"hundreds of polling places for women (polls were segregated to keep men and women from mingling publicly) did not even open in some areas where Taliban influence is high. Women also suffered discrimination and intimidation in some places in central and northern Afghanistan."*

In spite of *Women for Women International* staff in Afghanistan helping some two thousand women register to vote, the Country Director told the reporter that during the August election, *"the Afghan female electorate had no voice. Women complained but were ignored."* It was also reported that *"Afghan men often took votes from their wives and daughters 'on their behalf,' disenfranchising them by telling them it was unsafe for them to vote."* As a result, there is very little chance that conditions for women will improve in the next a few years.

Pakistan, 97% Muslim, is considered one of the worst offenders of women's rights in the Islamic world. Despite recent attempts by the Pakistani Government to adopt different UN treaties protecting women's rights, very little actual progress has been made. Domestic violence runs rampant and is so culturally entrenched that it remains underreported and virtually ignored by authorities. Marital rape is legal and other rape charges require the testimony of four Muslim men in good standing, making it almost impossible to press charges. If a Pakistani woman cannot provide the required testimony to prove she had been raped, she may then be charged with adultery. Such inhumane and impossible laws maintain the status quo of fear and repression and keep women's mouths shut.

Pakistani girls are often malnourished compared to the boys in their own families, and are uneducated and completely unprepared to enter the workforce. With the only work options being unskilled, low-paying labor, women are either financially dependent on husbands, or, if they head their own household, are crushingly poor. Education among women is limited to the upper class with the number of women in the workforce only about 15%.

In the Khyber tribal region, Pakistani Taliban leaders have issued a warning to the authorities against issuing national identity cards to women, claiming it to be an un-Islamic practice.

In March 2010 in neighboring **Bangladesh**, reports describe a 26-year-old mother beaten and bullied by her husband because he was unhappy she gave birth to a daughter instead of a son. This brutal man began putting drops of acid on different parts of his infant girl's body for five days and then began feeding her acid. This left the little girl, now nine years old, with physical as well as emotional scars. The mother complained to the police but charges were never filed. Finally, the mother and daughter ran away to find sanctuary at the *Acid Survivors' Foundation* hospital were the little girl has undergone several plastic surgeries on her mouth.

Another tale of Pakistani brutality, reported in the *Montreal Gazette* in May 2000, is the story of Zahida Perveen, whose face was severely deformed by her husband. *"He came home from the mosque and accused me of having a bad character... I told him it was not true, but he didn't believe me. He caught me and tied me up, and then he started cutting my face. He never said a word, except, 'This is your last night'."*

Women's groups in Pakistan are trying to make political changes by demanding that all legislative bodies reserve 1/3 of their seats for women. Hopes are that with more women in decision-making positions, structures will be created supporting their legal rights and financial autonomy. At the current time, there are virtually no such supportive structures in place. Ironically, Hijab does nothing to protect Pakistani women from being beaten, stared at in public, stalked by strange men and even raped. The Pakistani culture simply views women as sexual objects, whether modestly dressed or not. Without legal rights in their favor, Pakistani women have little chance of gaining social and sexual respect.

Despite having one of the world's largest Muslim populations, and in spite of the efforts of many Islamic groups over the last 50 years to amend its constitution with rules of Shari'a law, **Indonesia** remains a secular country. Nevertheless, in areas of condensed Muslim population, such as the northern tip of Sumatra, the local government specifically authorizes the practice of Shari'a law in conjunction with the secular civil and criminal laws.

Women under Shari'a law follow Hijab in addition to other Islamic rules.

The Indonesian Council of Ulama *[men of Islamic learning]* doesn't hold any real or binding power over women, but it continues to decree *fatwa's [Islamic decree]* which interfere with their personal lives. For example, in January 2010, *Muslimsdebate.com* reported on the council's Fatwa Commission forbidding the girls of the East Java boarding school from straightening their hair with a certain type of chemical treatment. The deputy secretary of the Fatwa Commission pronounced the hair treatment a *"breach of Islamic law...except for women who are married and have the permission of their husband."* The Fatwa committee in Indonesia has also banned women from riding in local taxis because of the possibility of their bodies touching the body of the male driver. As bizarre and humiliating as it sounds, women endure this type of personal violation of their own will and decisions every day.

Although the above examples seem somewhat petty, Islamic violence exists in Indonesia as well. A 2006 poll by *The Indonesia Survey Institute* showed an increasing rate of support for stoning adulterers as per Shari'a law and in October 2009, a young **Malaysian** woman was sentenced to caning for the crime of drinking a beer.

AFRICA

The exact number of Muslims in Africa is unknown, but Islam is this continent's largest religion. North and West Africa have the highest percentage of Muslims, but Islam's influence is rising quickly in central and eastern Africa as well.

African women have been the silent victims of twisted traditions intertwined with religious antiquities, keeping them under a dark cloud of poverty, illiteracy, and various forms of sexual mutilation from birth to death. Illiteracy ranks as high as 86% among **Sudani** girls and some 60-100% of the **Nigerian** women have endured genital mutilation. Most of the Nigerian states observe Shari'a law and, in addition to FGM, common practices include child marriage, rape, polygamy, and stoning for adultery. Because open dialogue about sex is considered immoral and taboo, women are unable to discuss the realities of their lives. According to Olayinka Koso-Thomas a native Nigerian doctor who has lived in Sierra Leone most of her life, *"In a country where an estimated 90 percent of women have undergone female genital mutilation, social pressures to conform can be overwhelming."*

In **Uganda**, physicians and lawmakers are attempting to criminalize FGM, but they fear that the ethnic communities will take the practice underground. Although Uganda has not banned FGM, they are hoping to educate the public about the health risks related to cutting.

A survey conducted by the United Nations and local organizations reports a high volume of rapes within Africa's refugee camps. Not only do refugee women live in fear of rape, but they often live in close proximity to their rapist, in constant fear of being raped again. Even living with family in a refugee camp doesn't guarantee protection; one young man heard his wife being raped by local thugs on her way to the toilet but was powerless to help for fear of losing his own life while defending hers.

It is shocking to read that many gang members carry knives with them in case they have to cut open their rape victim's vagina, which may still be stitched up from their circumcision.

Egyptian women have been the target of contentious clashes between the secular government's wish to restore women's rights to higher education and a less restricted dress code, and the Islamic extremists' desire to veil and segregate women and limit their attendance in universities. In January 2000, *BBC News* reported on a mother of two taking advantage of the Egyptian Parliament's recently approved law allowing women the right to file for divorce.

The *Middle East Times* reports that women in **Algeria** are the target of most of the country's crimes, but their government continues to ignore them.

CENTRAL ASIA & EUROPE

Europe's Muslim population numbers approximately 53 million and is estimated to double by 2020, while the non-Muslim population is reportedly shrinking at the same rate. Most of Europe's Muslims reside in Albania, Kosovo, Bosnia, and Herzegovina; Turkey,

Azerbaijan, and Kazakhstan remain Muslim majority countries. Western Europe's Muslim population is made up mostly of immigrants who have arrived over the last fifty years.

The situation for women varies, depending on the enforcement of Shari'a law by local Muslim authorities. For instance, the United Kingdom's prohibits the existence of Shari'a courts, but a 2009 report shows some 85 Shari'a courts in operation behind closed doors.

Their decisions are likely to be unfair to women and backed by intimidation. Rulings include:

- *That no Muslim woman may marry a non-Muslim man unless he converts to Islam and that any children of a woman who does should be taken from her until she marries a Muslim.*

- *Approval of "polygamous marriage and enforce a woman's duty to have sex with her husband on his demand."*
- *A male child belongs to the father after the age of seven, regardless of circumstances.*
  (http://en.wikipedia.org/wiki/Islam_in_Europe)

Even in Europe's secular nations, Muslim men continue killing their female relatives in the name of honor. Take the case of Hatun Aynur Sürücü, reported by *BBC News*, a twenty-three year old Turkish woman who was gunned down in front of her apartment in **Germany** by her youngest brother in February of 2005. Apparently, *"she had been married to her cousin eight years before in an arranged marriage, but had then run away – taking her five-year-old son with her."*

The German police hold a long list of Muslim women murdered by their male relatives. One woman was drowned in a bathtub, another stabbed by her husband in front of their 3-year-old daughter.

BBC News quoted on a social worker in Berlin who runs a center for runaways:

Every year dozens of women and girls, some as young as 13, run away to avoid arranged marriages – some in fear for their lives. Some were raped – by an uncle, by a cousin, even by the father – and when they should get married they are worried that someone will find out they're not a virgin anymore. They are afraid that they will be murdered. All these girls who come to us are locked in, in the house, by their families. They only go to school because they have to by law – otherwise they wouldn't be allowed.

They have to stay at home and cook, and care for the sisters and brothers.
The parents don't accept that the girl decides anything by herself.
(http://news.bbc.co.uk/2/hi/europe/4345459.stms)

Since 1996, the Turkish women's organization *Papatya,* has reported several honor killings in Germany. The Director of Britain's Prosecution Services reported that from 2004-05, *"at least a dozen honor killings"* had taken place in the United Kingdom.

In Turkey, police uncovered the body of a 16-year-old girl, who had been buried in a sitting position with her hands tied. The girl's father and grandfather buried her alive because she had been talking to boys, and these men wanted to reclaim their 'honor.' A February 2010 report from *Huffington Post* indicates that more than 200 of the annually reported murders in Turkey are honor killings.

Many European governments are taking a strong stand against Hijab in public places. The French Parliament has moved to ban the *Burqa* and other forms of full Islamic veiling in areas such as schools, hospitals, transit centers, and governmental offices. In January 2010, French President Nicolas Sarkozy announced *"In our country, we cannot accept that women be prisoners behind a screen, cut off from all social life, deprived of all identity. The Burqa is not a religious sign; it's a sign of subservience, a sign of debasement." (http://www.france24.com/en/category/tags-thematiques/burqa)*

Other European countries such as the Netherlands, Belgium, Denmark, Italy, Austria, and the UK already have laws, which ban the full Islamic veil or are considering implementing some rigorous laws against clothing that confines women's mobility and identity.

European lawmakers have also become more aware of Female Genital Mutilation (FGM), which has been performed on an estimated 500,000 African and Asian female immigrants and refugees in European countries. *IPS News* reported in February of 2010:

With hundreds of thousands of girls and women believed to be at risk of female genital mutilation (FGM) in Europe, rights groups have mounted a campaign to get EU leaders to stop what they see as a barbaric and dangerous procedure.

In order to avoid facing legal consequences in Europe, some Muslim parents take their daughters abroad during school holidays and carry on the circumcision in their home countries. Sometimes African doctors come to Europe to secretly perform FGM. Unfortunately, the problem seems to be much larger than originally estimated and that:

Systematic and repeated discussion of FGM is needed in communities where it is practiced. This has been shown to be the most effective method of reducing it. People involved in it need to be educated and fully informed about it. This is happening in Africa but something like this is lacking in Europe.

(http://www.ipsnews.net/news.asp?idnews=50359)

The Kosovo War of the late 1990 has led to tens of thousands of women being raped as a routine act of war. Even though that war is officially over, Kosovar women continue to suffer at the hands of the men who are supposedly on their side.

In March 2008, *The Los Angeles Times* published the story of Fatima, a 26-year-old Kosovar mother of three, who had been in and out of women's shelters for years. Her husband and father-in-law beat her severely on a regular basis for petty reasons such as asking for food or money to buy medicine for a sick child.

Sometimes she would go days without eating. Although Fatima's father was a landowner, he divided his property between his two sons and left his daughter with nothing. Penniless and without permission to work outside the house, Fatima had been trapped in a tiny house with her tyrannical husband and his father. The most recent shelter visit was hoped to be her last, and the shelter was searching for a permanent home for Fatima and her children. The shelter workers consider Fatima to be lucky, since they have seen numerous other women in her situation fall victim to sex trafficking.

The United Nations' 2000 review of the situation revealed that *"one-fourth of the female population of Kosovo suffered physical or psychological abuse; Kosovo police last year recorded 1,077 cases of domestic violence."* Women's advocates and social workers admit that, for every saved woman in Kosovo, there are many who do not make it.

THE UNITED STATES & CANADA

Even with a fast-growing Muslim population, the Canadian province of Quebec banned the face-covering *Niqab* in March 2010 with near unanimous support from the Canadian people. Apparently, even most Muslim Canadians shun *Niqab*, considering it too extreme a form of veiling. Across the other provinces of Canada, 4 out of 5 people are also opposed to the *Niqab*.

Even Muslim women living in the United States are not immune from honor killing. In November 2009, a young Iraqi woman living in Arizona was deliberately hit by her father's car, who claimed that she had become *'too Westernized'*. The twenty-year-old woman underwent spinal surgery but died from her injuries. Her father fled the country but he was later arrested and returned to stand trial in Arizona court. According to the county prosecutor, the father admitted to committing the crime: *"By his own admission, this was an intentional act and the reason was that his daughter had brought shame on him and his family."*

CHAPTER V

WOMEN AND INFERIORITY

.

*"Enlighten the people generally, and tyranny and oppressions of body
and mind will vanish like evil spirits at the dawn of day."*
Thomas Jefferson

MYTHS AND TRUTHS

The inequality between men and women originated thousands of
years ago. The *male-dominated* class based society was characterized in
the areas of private property ownership, the state, the church, and a
family system serving men's interest.

*Male supremacy, according to this myth, is not a social phenomenon at a
particular stage of history, but a natural law. Men, it is claimed, are
endowed by nature with superior physical and mental attributes. It is set
forth as an equally immutable axiom that women are socially inferior*

because they are naturally *inferior to men. And what is the proof? They are the mothers! Nature, it is claimed, has condemned the female sex to an inferior status. (Reed, 1954)*

However, it is not nature, but society, which has stripped women of their class status. In primitive societies, the perceived superiority between men and women was non-existent and if anything, women were social and cultural leaders. Oriana Fallaci[1] claims that, *you cannot survive if you do not know the past.* Let us briefly examine the past. Primitive social cultures were established based on matriarchy, which clearly as indicated by name, was organized and led by women. Women, blessed with the organs and role of childbearing transformed the animal kingdom into civilization and were held in high regard in society.

Women, as mothers and nurturers began the first labor and production of humanity. In addition to farming and seed gathering, women learned how to co-exist in the society by inventing dialogue

---

[1] Oriana Fallaci (29 June 1929 – 15 September 2006) was an Italian journalist, author, and political interviewer. A former partisan during World War II, she had a long and successful journalistic career.

and tools to communicate. Every element of the universe holds its own individual functionality. Women and men are neither superior nor inferior to each other. In primitive societies, men and women learned to divide their responsibilities by assigning women to food gathering, protecting the children, invent farming tools and farming, hunting small game, domesticating livestock, and preserving food for future consumption, while men as hunters left home to hunt wild life. As cited in *The Myth of Women's Inferiority*, Alexander Goldenweiser in *Anthropology* said; *everywhere the sustenance of this part of the household is more regularly and reliably provided by the efforts of the homebound woman than by those of her roving hunter husband or son,* (sometimes they came back empty handed).

Women, upon discovery of fire – also discovered all the basic cooking tools and techniques as well as making pots with clay. In *The Myth of Women's Inferiority*, Evelyn Reed explains, "*Fire was the tool of tools in primitive society. And it was the women, who developed all the early industries, who likewise uncovered the uses of fire as a tool in their industries. The first industrial life of women centered around the food supply. Preparing, conserving and preserving food required the invention of all the necessary collateral equipment: containers, utensils, ovens, storage houses, etc. The women were the builders of the first caches, granaries and storehouses for the provisions.*" *(1954)*

Women learned how to extract poison out of certain inedible plants and prepare them medicinally. Dr. Dan McKenzie in *The Infancy of Medicine*, as cited in *The Myth of Women's Inferiority*, refers to hundreds of homeopathic remedies discovered by primitive women with some of them still in use.

Textile and weaving are also among women's significant discoveries, leading to the basket industry.

Despite historians, glorifying men's hunting ability, women performed the tedious art of leather making. As cited in *The Myth of Women's Inferiority*, Robert H. Lowie in *An Introduction to Social Anthropology* describes the earliest form of labor practiced by the Ona women of Tierra del Fuego. After the men hunters brought back a guanaco hide, "... *kneels on the stiff rawhide and laboriously scrapes off the fatty tissue and the transparent layer below it with her quartz blade. After a while, she kneads the skin piecemeal with her fists, going over the whole surface repeatedly and often bringing her teeth into play until it is softened. If the hair is to be taken off, that is done with the same scraper.*"

From beginning of time, women were involved with housing and architecture. As cited by Reed in *The Myth of Women's Inferiority*, Robert S. Briffault, a French anthropologist and surgeon refer to the Australian huts, the American Indian skin lodges, and nomadic Central Asian Yurta, as evidence of construction works originated by women. There are traces of elaborate, complex, and dome like Yurta with interiors divided into several compartments, mostly products of the Turkoman women. The *pueblos* of New Mexico and Arizona also testify to women's highly developed architectural ability.

Briffault mentions that the beauty of the churches and buildings that women and girls built for Spanish priests who were settling among the Pueblo Indians amazed them. They wrote back to their countrymen; *"No man has ever set his hand to the erection of a house ... These buildings have been erected solely by the women, the girls, and the young men of the mission; for among these people it is the custom that the women build the houses."*

The notion of women who are looked upon by men as frail and fragile is nothing more than male fear of female well-rounded strength. According to anthropologists, *E. Chapple & C. Coon*, as cited in *The Myth of Women's Inferiority*, there are still women in Ona tribes of Tierra del Fuego, carrying heavy loads of up to 100 pounds as they move through campsites. Men on the other hand, approach their carried weight limits, at 60 pounds. I recall my own childhood memory of our family trips to Iraqi cities as I watched the Arabian nomadic women coming to town from the desert. They always carried well over 70 pounds of copper and steel pots upon their heads. I remember them looking straight ahead and walking fast, almost as though they were under hypnosis. As a child, I tried to read their minds detecting their anger or remorse at the abundances of lazy men sitting on sidewalk cafes drinking sweet tea in clear glasses and puffing on water pipes, while babbling political nonsense to escape their boredom.

Briffault writes: *"The fanciful opinion that women are oppressed in savage societies was partly due to the complacency of civilized man, and partly to the fact that the women are seen to work hard. Wherever women were seen engaged in laborious toil, their status was judged to be one of slavery and oppression. No misunderstanding could be more profound."*

Women had to learn everything first hand and the hard way. They learned from nature and literally the birds, the bees, the plants, and the spiders. Such depth of insight and humility allowed women to carry on with observing, absorbing, learning, teaching, and creating. Women however, during the first social development brought humanity forward and away from animal kingdom. Men, on the other hand relied on women's gained knowledge and as Evelyn Reed describes, *"Although it required hundreds of thousands of years for the women to lay down these social foundations, it is precisely because they laid them down so firmly and so well that it has taken less than 4,000 years to bring civilization to its present estate."* (1954)

Up to today, no scientific or rational explanation has emerged that explains men's superiority and women's inferiority. Nevertheless, at some point in the past, an unjust reversal among the sexes has taken place moving us forward to today.

"The very conditions that brought about the emancipation of men brought about the overthrow of the matriarchy and the enslavement of women. As social production came into the hands of men, women were dispossessed from productive life and driven back to their biological function of maternity. Men took over the reins of society and founded a new social system, which served their needs. Upon the ruins of the matriarchy, class society was born...." At last - *"To understand these historical facts is to avoid the pitfalls of arbitrary judgment made through emotion or prejudice. And to understand these facts is to explode the myth that women are naturally inferior to men."* (Reed, 1954)

Why Inferior Feeling?

In the Muslim world, men have displayed a two-faced, double standard approach toward women. On the one hand, men *honor* women as their mothers and wives ready to lay down their lives and die for them. On the other hand, they *shame* their mothers and wives for a potential risk of rape or conquering by men that are more powerful. This conflictive attitude has infected societies affecting members of all ages. The results are a series of senseless hostilities, bloodshed, and absurdities toward women and girls. Although the discussion is true for almost all cultures and religions, Islam, with its ideology, culture, and Shari'a law has created a means to legitimize the exclusion of women from decision-making authority, or any voice at all. The translation of Ayatollah Khomeini's speeches on women addresses them as "deceitful creatures", easily influenced by the forces of evil. The Prophet Muhammad claimed that a majority of women belong to the hell-fire. Throughout history, violence against women has become the norm rather than the exception. Most men at any age, trained to recall being a victim of physical or verbal abuse as opposed to women who are more likely compelled to forgive and forget. Women have even been trained to qualify the degree of abuse before reacting to it. For example, was that only shoving and shouting? Oh, that must be alright, since it didn't escalate to hitting and punching!!

As long as violence toward women originates from men, it is also logical to assume it is leading to a belief system that categorizes women as *inferior.*

"Whether it comes from a despotic sovereign or an elected president, from a murderous general or a beloved leader, I see power as an inhuman and hateful phenomenon." (Oriana Fallaci)

* * * * *

In our modern times, injustice in the name of Islam continues to keep women silent, terrified, and oppressed. The issue of Hijab, and all that it implies, is a current one, and a global one as well. It is crucial that those of us who are capable of making a difference attempt to do something tangible by supporting any person or organization focused on expanding educational opportunities to the Islamic women of the world.

CHAPTER VII

LOOKING FORWARD

"Believe you can and you're halfway there."

Theodore Roosevelt

After reading the first manuscript of this book, my daughter, wrote:

It left me yearning to know what could truly change the situation for these women? I wonder, how can education and self-respect be spread to these women, but in a way that is also respectful of their cultural context? It is not appropriate to take Western ideas and push them onto people who are not prepared to accept them. But rather to use ideas that are appropriate, to allow women to come to their own conclusions, to expose them to better visions of who they can be and how they can interact in a more positive manner with their world. Is this possible? And is there a way to convince the men that this would be for their ultimate benefit as well? I can understand why Muslim men would be threatened by a Western cultural takeover...but is there a way to show them that women can fulfill themselves as real human beings and be valuable life partners, while at the same time not falling into Western materialist traps?

HOPE THROUGH EDUCATION

The story of Mukhtar Mai[1], a Pakistani woman held captive in a tribal dispute and gang-raped on the orders of her village's tribal elders, shook the consciousness of her nation as well that of freedom lovers everywhere. She survived the ordeal and, with much encouragement and global support, was able to rise above the self-pity, pain, and suffering by making a conscious decision to fight back against the corrupt local government. In addition, she turned her battle into a crusade against the hazards of illiteracy by demanding

---

[1] Mukhtaran Bibi, born c. 1972, is a Pakistani woman from the village of Meerwala, in the rural *tehsil* (county) of Jatoi of the Muzaffargarh District of Pakistan. Mukhtar Mai suffered a gang rape as a form of honor revenge, on the demands of tribesmen — or by some accounts, on the orders of a *panchayat* (tribal council) — of a local Mastoi Baloch clan that was richer and more powerful than Mukhtaran's clan, the Gujjar Tatla.

that the government build a school in her village. Mukhtar Mai made education and literacy for girls in the village a possibility.

In the book of Mukhtar Mai's story, *In the Name of Honor*, Marie-Therese Cuny explains how Mukhtar knew that, ultimately, the way to win the struggle against the local men and their ridiculous laws was through education. She became more certain when she realized the local police had manipulated her rape story by writing a different report than what she told them and was doubly astonished when the judge admitted that the written report, which showed her thumbprint signature and was given to the judge by the police, was entirely different from her verbal statement.

A woman is nothing more than an object of exchange, from birth to marriage. According to custom, she has no right... that is how I was raised, and no one ever told me that Pakistan had a constitution, laws, and rights written down in a book. I have never seen a lawyer or a judge. I know absolutely nothing about the official justice, reserved for wealthy and educated people. (Cuny, 2002)

She ranked women as lower than a goat tied to a tree. Men, on the other hand, were positioned with the ultimate authority in society, and would tell women: *"...you will say only what I'm telling you to say, because it's in your best interest..."*

After all of Mukhtar's hardships, it was her school that brought a real sense of pride into her life.

Whenever I hear a student ... chanting the multiplication tables and the English alphabet, I feel that my life has real meaning. Soon there will also be history and geography lessons. My girls, my little sisters, will be learning the same things that boys study. (Cuny, 2002)

Stories like Mukhtar Mai's are an exception to the rule, since in such backward societies, all that women learn is to keep silent, not to disturb anyone, and not to make their presence known to men. Male rulers desire a woman's total silence, and total submission. Women have been deprived from expressing their opinions and making intimate decisions about their lives.

Mukhtar sadly described meeting a battered woman who came to see her after learning about her bravery and says:

...she simply shows me her face, discreetly, shamefully. And I understand. Acid has eaten half of it away. And she can't even cry anymore. Who did this? Her husband. Why? He used to beat her, she wasn't serving him fast enough to suit him. (Cuny, 2002)

That woman was only one of many cases and there was not much Mukhtar could do for her. She expressed her sympathy and gave her some money in hopes that she'd leave her husband and go back to her family, assuming they would accept her.

EDUCATION AND AWARENESS

It is imperative that we educate our children from early on and help them to develop their critical thinking abilities. After all, it is up to our children to lead the way and find the best solution to this and other problems. In the case of Islam's treatment of women, solutions must be found that are culturally suitable and aligned with local custom.

Today, millions of women and girls, mainly Muslims, are illiterate. The cycle repeats as long as uneducated girls grow up to be unprepared mothers without parenting competency. Self-awareness, education, and understanding of the opportunities available to young girls helps reshape their view and ultimately breaks the paralysis of cultural dogma and the imposition of tribal, religious, and local beliefs. Teaching young boys societal and citizenship responsibilities will help them see the opposite sex as valued members of society.

If the answer lies in education, then an immense amount of education is needed at different levels, spread between the Eastern and Western worlds. I am personally ashamed for not having prior knowledge about female circumcision until I started researching these women's issues. We must continue talking about these issues and educating ourselves about the horror, these women experience in their daily lives.

Once proper education settles its way into the hearts and minds of such youngsters, the changing of antiquated and brutal laws against women will be the next logical step towards embracing the principles of humanity. The road ahead is treacherous and the goal seems at times unattainable; however, different societies will arrive at their realizations and step forward at a different pace.

Education can be the beginning of justice in the Islamic world.
(Siteresources.worldbank.org/INTECD/Images/ecd.gif)

We should not depend on the women themselves to carry the banner of education since most women who know of these practices are also stumbling around their shame and embarrassment. They need champions to tell them they are not at fault for being born

female and that it is unacceptable to tolerate brutality from men. We must remain educated about current affairs affecting women's lives across the globe. This awareness heightens our consciousness, which spills over to our households, neighborhood, schools, and all of society, making crimes against women intolerable.

POLITICAL SOLUTIONS

According to Mrs. Benazir Bhutto, twice President of Pakistan, there is a clear connection in contemporary times between economic justice and political liberty. As long as the subject of women's rights has not been resolved, there will be a hole in humanity's core Democracy is the first step toward humanity's liberation.

Women can achieve such liberation through open dialogue, education of both sexes, and female empowerment through economic and political stability. Men in these societies must first learn to recognize women as human beings instead of objects, and then see them as friends and partners. Women, on the other hand, must learn to recognize their strength and power as people in society. As mothers, women are capable of teaching their boys the proper way to behave, as they become future men.

Perhaps what men fear the most is that women might decide to stop becoming pregnant and delivering babies; that they might stop being the peacemakers and Earth nurturers? Instead of expressing their appreciation toward women, however, men force their manhood on them through violence and by keeping them pregnant, dependent, helpless, and terrified. That is one way of settling the question of authority; hypnotizing an opponent with one's delusional power, rendering them unable to think rationally. This sum up the fate of millions of women in Islamic countries: they are dizzy from being afraid and constantly beaten up, wrapped up in an ancient culture full of suppression and superstition.

Progressive nations shamefully continue their business-as-usual attitude with the fundamentalist heads of such nations and avoid the fact that men in those societies brutalize women everyday, looking the other way and excusing such behavior as the culture and traditional way of life.

Benazir Bhutto[1] spoke at the 2001 Council of Indian Industry in New Delhi, India and asserted:

By your focus on the essential rights of women in society, you support the voice of the powerless, the exploited, and the abused. For women, despite the strides taken in the last century, are still the most powerless and exploited group in the world community. Furthermore, the cause of women is God's most noble cause, the cause of justice, equality and life… It is impossible to separate women's rights from human rights… (Speaker-Yuan, 2005)

----

[1] Benazir Bhutto, Pakistan's Prime Minister from 1988-90 and 1993-96, (21, June 1953 – 27 December 2007). Daughter of former Prime Minister Zulfikar Ali Bhutto.

Depending on the flavor of the day and the government's political vicissitudes, serious women's issues are set aside as belonging to the domain of Islamic rules or cultural practices. However, it doesn't matter if the brutality is labeled Islamic or cultural, it is still dehumanizing. The UN Secretary General Ban Ki-Moon emphasizes, *"Violence against women is an abomination. I'd like to call it a crime against humanity."*

World leaders need to recognize that violence against women is a human rights issue, and if there is a growing fear of rocking the boat between the nations, in my opinion, it is already too late: the ship is already sinking, abandoning millions of women and children in darkness.

Pressure must be put on our own lawmakers and heads of states to demand gender equality and a crackdown on crimes against women around the world. The American concept of 'separation of Church and State' has been, over the centuries, adopted in several other countries and today, more than ever, we are obligated to find a way to extract Shari'a law from the constitutions of the Islamic fundamentalist governments and encourage the practice of religion as a personal affair.

In the book, *Introducing Issues with Opposing Viewpoints: Islam,* the author refers to Azam Kamguian's[1] suggestion that instead of trying to modernize Islam by masking its oppressive behavior toward women, we must *"cage it, just as humanity caged Christianity two centuries ago. Islam must become subordinate to secularism and the secular State."* (Friedman, 2006)

The Taliban and the Ayatollah alike are taken very seriously when they declare war against non-Muslims, and certain developing countries are scrutinized for their nuclear capabilities, but hardly the world leaders have directly challenged the very real danger of the Islamic leaders' power over issues related to women and young girls. We rarely hear about the severity of the problem.

The collective of male leaders, cautious of rocking the boat between the Islamic fanatics and their own agenda, fail to do the right thing. They must demand justice and equality for women from the tyrants. These women and girls are not able to achieve such an enormous counter cultural task on their own unless they receive profound backing from the other half of the earth's population: men and boys.

---

[1] Azam Kamguian is an Iranian writer and women's rights activist. She was born in 1958 and started her political activities as a socialist in 1976.

Leaders are needed who can take the bull by the horns and fight the disgraceful and infectious disease of male supremacy. There must be a healing of the deep-rooted wounds inflicted on women and innocent infant girls.

Progressive governments and organizations must be vigilant in feeling the pulse of disadvantaged nations for their receptivity to change and move quickly as such environments become ready for reform. The road is long and the work is tedious, but it must be done, so that the centuries old cruelty can no longer break the bodies and gentle spirits of countless women and girls.

The unveiling of woman and her emancipation from the shackles of cruel Koranic law should not be seen as impiety and ungodliness. Islam can only benefit from the removal of these vestiges of a medieval past, which have blocked progress in so many countries for too long. (Hekmat, 1997)

APPENDIX

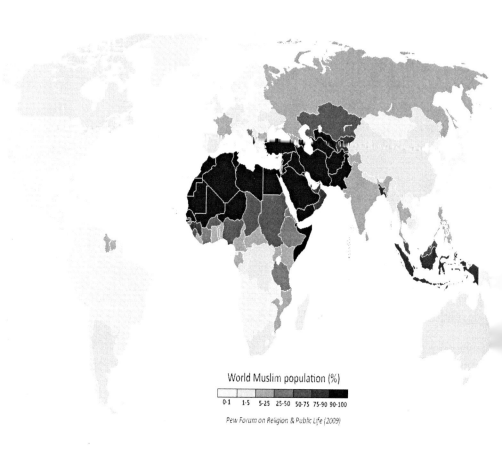

World Muslim population (%)

0-1   1-5   5-25   25-50   50-75   75-90   90-100

Pew Forum on Religion & Public Life (2009)

COUNTRIES WITH THE HIGHEST MUSLIM
POPULATION

	Estimated 2009 Population	Percentage of Population that is Muslim	Percentage of World Muslim Population
Indonesia	202,867.000	88.2%	12.9%
Pakistan	174,082.000	96.3	11.1
India	160,945.000	13.4	10.3
Bangladesh	145,312.000	89.6	9.3
Egypt	78,513.000	94.6	5.0
Iran	73,777.000	99.4	4.7
Turkey*	73,619.000	~98	4.7
Algeria	34,199.000	98.0	2.2
Morocco*	31,993.000	~99	~2

*Data for Turkey and Morocco come primarily from general population surveys, which are less reliable than censuses or large-scale demographic and health surveys.

Reference: Pew Research Center's Forum on Religion & Public Life • Mapping the Global Muslim Population, October 2009, www.pewforum.org.

GLOSSARY OF TERMS

Burqa – An enveloping outer garment worn only by women in some Islamic traditions for the purpose of hiding a female's body when out in public. The entire body is shrouded by this garment, with only some netting in front of the eyes to see through.

Chador – The Iranian form of Hijab, which consists of a black cloth cloaked around the body, showing only the face and hands.

Female Genital Mutilation – Also known as FGM or female circumcision, this is the practice of cutting away the clitoris, and sometimes the inner and outer labia as well.

Hadith – The Prophet's sayings and actions are recorded separately in collections known as *Hadith*.

Hijab – The general term for the Islamic head covering.

Hijrah – (هِجْرَة) is the migration of the Prophet Muhammad and his followers from Mecca to the city of Medina in AD 622.

Houris – The beautiful virgins of the Koranic Paradise. From Persian *hūri,* from Arabic *hūr,* plural of *haurā'* woman with dark eyes.

Infidel – A non-believer of Islam.

Iranian Special Religious Patrol – Men and women of the Islamic Revolutionary Guard enforcing government mandated Hijab in public.

Jihad – A religious duty of Muslims. The word *jihād* is a noun meaning "struggle." Jihad appears frequently in the Qur'an and common usage as the idiomatic expression "striving in the way of *Allah*". A person engaged in jihad is called a *mujahid,* the plural is mujahideen.

Jinn – A supernatural being in Islam.

Kabul – (archaic Caubul), The capital and largest city of Afghanistan, located in Kabul Province. According to a 2009 census, it has a population of 3,568,500.

Kharabat – Farsi word for brothel.

The Koran (Qur'an) – All the verses revealed to the Prophet Mohammad are compiled in the <u>Koran</u>.

Messenger of *Allah* – Islam claims that in the year 610 AD, Mohammad, while on a retreat at Mount Hira for meditation, received his first revelation from the Archangel Gabriel.

Mohammed Omar – Known as *Mullah* Omar, the leader of the <u>Taliban</u> of <u>Afghanistan</u> from 27 September 1996 – 13 November 2001, under the official title of *Head of the Supreme Council*. He was launched into the spotlight after the terror in September 11, 2001.

Mullah – A Muslim trained in the doctrine and law of Islam; the head of a mosque.

Mut'a – Meaning 'joy' in Arabic; similar to *Seegheh* in Farsi, which means temporary marriage.

Niqab – A veil which covering the face and showing only the eyes. It is part of the Hijab dress code worn by some <u>Muslim</u> women.

Prophet Mohammad – Mohammad was born around the year 570 in the city of Mecca (c. 570 – 632). He is the founder of Islam.

Pahlavi Dynasty – The Pahlavi Dynasty ruled Iran from the crowning of <u>Reza Shah Pahlavi</u> in <u>1925</u> to the overthrow of his son <u>Mohammad Reza Pahlavi</u> in the <u>Iranian Revolution</u> of <u>1979</u>.

Qum – (<u>Persian</u>: ﻗﻢ, also known as Qom or Ghom) is a city in <u>Iran</u>. It lies 156 kilometres (97 mi) by road southwest of <u>Tehran</u> and is the capital of <u>Qum Province</u>. It has an estimated population of 1,042,309 in 2005. It is situated on the banks of the <u>Qum River</u>.

Resaleh – *Resaleh Towzih al-Masa'el*, also *Risaleh Towzih al Masa'il* aka Questions Clarified. This book is a collection of almost 2900 questions by, and answers for, pious traditional Shi'a on how to be good Muslims. Almost all of them (80%) are about personal behavior, ritual purity, or the five pillars of Islam.

Seegheh – *See Mut'a.*

Shari'a Law – The Islamic system of law and the totality of the Islamic way of life. Shari'a law is based on the Koran and the *Hadiths*.

Shiite – Follower of the Shia branch of Islam, which considers Ali, the cousin of Mohammad, and his descendants to be the Prophet Mohammad's true successors.

Sura – A chapter in The Qur'an (Koran).

Tafsir - (Arabic: ر يسفت, *tafsīr*, "interpretation") is the Arabic word for commentary, usually of the Qur'an.

Taliban – A Sunni Islamic political movement that governed Afghanistan from 1996 until they were overthrown in late 2001 during "Operation Enduring Freedom."

Zoroastrianism – The religious system founded by Zoroaster and set forth in the Avesta, teaching the worship of Ahura Mazda in the context of a universal struggle between the forces of light and of darkness.

REFERENCES

Abdul-Ghafur, Saleemah - book editor, (2005). Living Islam Outloud: American Muslim women speak.

Akeel, Maha (2005). Female Circumcision: Weight of tradition perpetuates a dangerous practice. Arab News, (20th of March). Retrieved January 6, 2009 from <http://www.arabnews.com>

Armstrong, Sally (2002). Veiled Threat – The Hidden Power of the Women of Afghanistan.

Cuny, Marie-Therese (2006). In the Name of Honor: A Memoir, Mukhtar Mai. Translated by Linda Coverdale.

Darabi, Parvin & Thomson, Romin, P., (1999). Rage Against the Veil: The Courageous Life and Death of an Islamic Dissident.
Evans, Mike (2009). Jimmy Carter: The Liberal Left & World Chaos.

Execution of a Teenage Girl. (2006, July 27). One Minute World News [Television documentary team]. UK: BBC News. Retrieved July 6, 2009 from <http://news.bbc.co.uk>

Female Circumcision (Genital Mutilation, FGM). from D@dalos, The International UNESCO Education Server for Civic, Peace and Human Rights Education, Retrieved January 8, 2009 <http://www.dadalos.org/int/Menschenrechte/Grundkurs_MR3/frauenrecht e/warum/beschneidung.htm>

Female Circumcision Threatens Girls in Germany (2004, April). Deutsche Welle, Germany's international broadcaster. Retrieved January 8, 2009 from <http://www.dw-world.de/dw/article/0,1564,1188662,00.html>

Friedman, Lauri, S. - book editor, (2006). Introducing Issues with Opposing Viewpoints: Islam.
Hekmat, Anwar (1997). Women and the Koran – The Status of Women in Islam.

Hijab: Personal Choice Not State Law. Insight Publication, (February 10, 2008). Retrieved December of 2008 from

<http://blog.lsinsight.org/2008/02/Hijab-personal-choice-not-state-law.html>

Hirsi Ali, Ayaan (2004). The Caged Virgin – An Emancipitation Proclamation for Women and Islam. Published: Netherlands, 2004 & First Free Press edition, 2006.

Hurley, Jennifer A. - book editor, (2001). Islam – Opposing Viewpoints.

International Women's Day (03/07/2000). UNICEF Executive Director Carol Bellamy speech. Retrieved December of 2008 from <http://www.unicef.org>

Kar, Mehrangiz (1387). A Research About Violence Against Women in Iran. From its original language, Farsi. *Note: The Iranian year 1387 equals the Gregorian year 2008-2009.*

Khan, Muhsin, M. (Translator). Introduction to Translation of Sahih Bukhari. Copyright 2007 – 2009, CMJE and the University of Southern California. Volume 1, Book 6, Number 301.

Lord Byron Quotes: English romantic poet and satirist, 1788-1824. Retrieved June 18, 2009 from <www.brainyquote.com>

Merriam Webster Dictionary (1980). Retrieved January 6, 2009 from <http://www.merriam-webster.com/dictionary/Hijab>

Moore, Matthew & Karuni, Rompies (2004). In the Cut. Sydney Morning Herald, (13th of January). Retrieved January 6, 2009 from <http://www.smh.com.au/articles/2004/01/12/107387776014 7.html>

Motahari, Morteza (1365). The Issue of Hijab. From the original Farsi. *Note: The Iranian year 1365 equals the Gregorian year 1987.*

Narrated Abu Said Al-Khudri. Retrieved July 16, 2009 from, <http://www.usc.edu/schools/college/crcc/engagement/resou rces/texts/muslim/hadith/bukhari/sbtintro.html>

Parshall, Phil & Julie (2002). Lifting the Veil – The World of Muslim Women.

Rahnavard, Zahra, Dr. (1986). Beauty of Concealment and Concealment of Beauty. English translation by: Dr. Sayyid Ali Raza, Naqvi. Cultural Consulate of the Islamic Republic of Iran: Islamabad, Pakistan. Retrieved 2008 from http://www.al-islam.org/beautyofconcealment/

Reed, Evelyn (1954). The Myth of Women's Inferiority. *Fourth International* (Spring 1954), vol.15 No. 2.

Sasson, Jean, P. (1992). Princess – A True Story of Life Behind the Veil in Saudi Arabia.

Speaker-Yuan, Margaret - editor, (2005). Women in Islam.

Spray, Lisa (2001). Heart's Surprise – A Personal Reconciliation of Women's Rights and the Quran and Islam.

Tafsir Ibn Kathir. Quran Tafsir. Retrieved July 17, 2009 from <http://www.qtafsir.com>

The Free Dictionary by Farlex (2009). Retrieved June 18, 2009 from <http://www.thefreedictionary.com/Hijab>

The Position of Women from the Viewpoint of Imam Khomeini. The Institute for Compilation and Publication of Imam Khomeini's Works (International Affairs Division). Translated by: Juliana Shaw & Behrooz Arezoo. Proofread and typeset by: Mansoor L. Limba.1st Printing: Autumn 2001.

The Sayings of Ayatollah Khomeini: Resaleh-Tozeeholmasael. 1st ed., from the original Farsi. Hafez Publication (unknown date). Tehran, Iran.

The Sayings of Ayatollah Khomeini: Tahrirolvasyleh. 4th ed., 1990. Qom, Iran. Retrieved December of 2008 from <http://ethnikoi.org/iran.html>

UN Unveils Network of Men to Fight Abuse of Women. The BBC News (November 25, 2009). Retrieved November of 2009 from <http://news.bbc.co.uk>

Various Questions (2) Answered by Shaykh Gibril Haddad. Living Islam – Islamic Tradition. (October 21, 2005). Retrieved July 17, 2009 from <http://www.livingislam.org>